A FINGER IN THE PIE

A Bruegel Mystery

Author's note

For the sake of the story I have situated Bruegel's paintings *Peasant Wedding, Massacre of the Innocents* and *Proverbs* in the Antwerp Museum of Fine Arts, when in fact the former two are in Vienna (Kunsthistorisches Museum) and the latter in Berlin (Gemäldegalerie). Bruegel's biographical data are for the most part fictional.

A FINGER IN THE PIE

A Bruegel Mystery

Luc Verreth

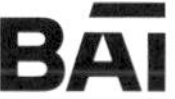

Every puppy should have a boy

- Erma Bombeck -

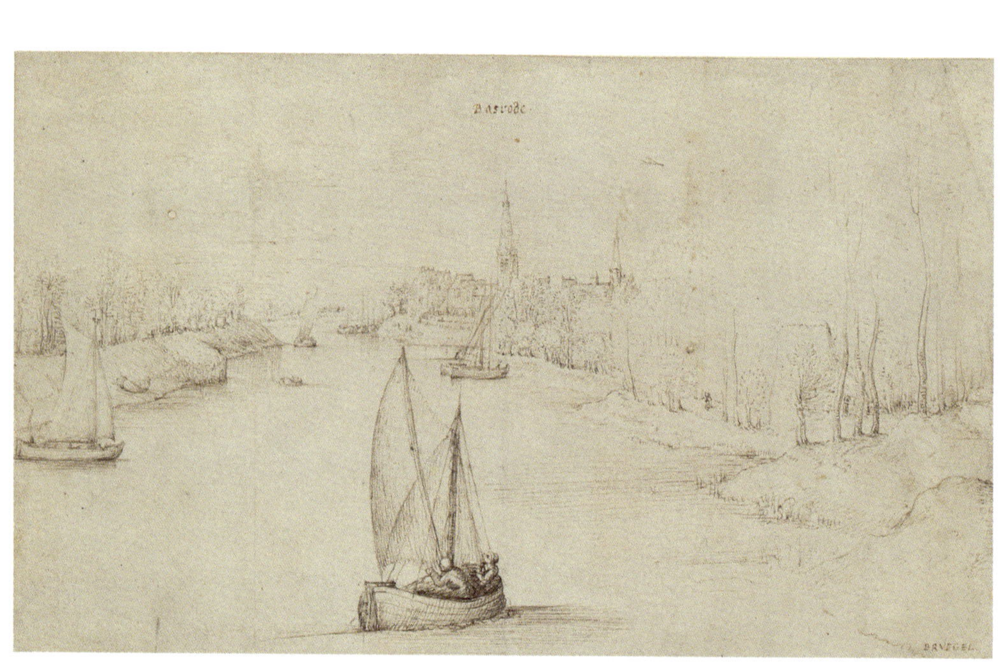
Basrode
BRVEGEL

Antwerp, 1557

On the banks of the river Scheldt Pieter collected some flat pebble stones. He wanted to make a dog tag for the puppy he got from Hieronymus Cock. Publisher Cock had a litter of Belgian shepherd dogs to get rid of and he gave one to Pieter in exchange for a drawing.

Back home in Kaasstraat, in the attic room he rented since he had recently moved to Antwerp, Pieter found the puppy asleep on the bed.

'Wake up, doggie. I've brought you something,' he said, picking out a beautiful black stone. The little dog woke up and came over on its wobbly legs. It had a striking white spot on its chest. 'I'll make you a nice collar so that Mayken can see what you're called.'

Mayken was the daughter of his master in the Antwerp painters' guild. She turned twenty the next day. Pieter fancied her and the puppy was her birthday gift.

'What shall we call you, little mongrel? Does Max sound all right to you? Max and Mayken. I like that.'

So he engraved MAX on the black stone and the year 1557 on the backside. He drilled a little hole in the stone and put a leather strap through it. As he tied the collar around the puppy's neck, the black stone ended up snug in the middle of the white spot on its chest.

'It fits,' Pieter said.

Then he chose another pebble stone, a grey one, and put the name REX on it. That collar was for publisher Cock, who'd said he wanted to keep one puppy for himself.

The next day the collar with the black stone was missing. Some way or another little Max had managed to get it off and make it disappear. Pieter searched his room in vain. He didn't have time to make a new collar. In fact, he was late as it was. 'We'll have to make do without it.' He took the puppy in his arms and went out.

Antwerp, today

I'm walking my son to school. Daan is in the first grade. He's small for his age and redheaded, just like me. As usual we make a short stop at the old-fashioned pet shop in Schildersstraat and have a look at the puppies in the shop window.

'I'm getting a puppy when I'm six,' he's been telling everyone for years. 'My daddy got one too at six, but his dog was killed in an accident... and so were his parents,' he always adds bluntly.

As usual I get the paper on my way home. *Prince Albert's to be flattened* it says on the front page. I can't believe it! Prince Albert boarding school razed to the ground. I'd spent a year there when I was twelve, sent there by my father's sister, aunt Jo. After my parents were killed, she became my guardian and I moved in with her, bringing my dog Max.

Aunt Jo and her cat Minou lived in a narrow little house in Kaasstraat which had a centuries-old façade but no garden. From day one Max and Minou were like cat and dog. Trying to avoid both Minou and aunt Jo, I spent a lot of time in the attic with Max. The first time there he was very agitated, sniffing in every nook and cranny. As he came to the old chimney he started to dig, whining softly, his claws scraping the ancient wooden floor. I went over to find out what had gotten him so excited. There was a crack between the chimney and the floor, wide enough to get two fingers in, something was there. I pulled carefully and out came a leather strap with a black pebble stone attached to it. Max yelped as I let him sniff at it. Then I took a closer look at the stone. It had a number on it, 1557, surely, that couldn't be the year 1557? That would make the thing four centuries old. As I turned the stone over, the name MAX jumped out at me.

'Would you believe it? It's got your name on it, Max.' He wagged his tail expectantly. 'You want me to hang it around your neck?' He barked. But as I tried to pull the old leather strap over his head, it broke. I looked around the room for a piece of twine or some such thing and spotted a pair of sturdy walking shoes. They had brightly coloured nylon shoelaces, long and strong. I put one through the hole in the stone and tied it around Max's neck in such a way that the black pebble rested smack in the middle of the white spot on his chest.

For a year aunt Jo and I did our best to get along. Then she came up with the idea of boarding school.

'But what about Max?' I asked.

She'd already worked out a solution. There was this jeweller she knew who could make good use of a watch dog. 'He lives quite close to the school,' she said. 'So, you can take Max for walks in the adjacent park whenever you want.' That won me over.

Prince Albert's wasn't the type of boarding school you get to see in films, looming mansions with a labyrinth of dark corridors that are lit up by lightning. Behind Prince Albert's imposing façade was an airy building that gave on to the park. Life there wasn't exactly princely but the proximity of Max made up for it.

For a while aunt Jo's plan seemed to work out until one day Max slipped out of the shop between a client's legs, ran into the street and was killed by a car. I only found out about it the next day as I came to take Max for a walk. I never got to see the dead dog. That was probably for the best.

'I'm terribly sorry,' the jeweller said, 'but there was no stopping him.'

I still believe Max wanted to go and find me.

'I thought you might want to have this,' the man said. He gave me Max's dog tag. I put it around my neck and returned to Prince Albert's, which suddenly looked even gloomier than boarding schools in films do. I cut myself off from everything and everyone. I was twelve and miserable as hell.

And then, early May 1989, a discovery in the Antwerp Museum of Fine Arts sent a shockwave around the world. The so-called Bruegel Mystery was frontline news for a couple of weeks. Eventually the whole thing ended as strangely and suddenly as it had started. The riddle was never solved and the story faded into oblivion.

But the news that Prince Albert's is about to be demolished, has stirred up old memories in me and I suddenly realize it's exactly thirty years since it all happened. I'm almost home, just passing the Museum, which finally got rid of the scaffolding and will soon re-open its doors. Four hundred and fifty years after his death Bruegel will once again be the focus of attention. A prestigious exhibition will attract crowds of people, but never, I daresay, as many as thirty years ago, when the world media invaded the museum square and people lined the surrounding streets to see the wonder with their own eyes.

By the time I open my front door, my mind is set. Now that the walls of Prince Albert's will come down, the moment has come to tear down the walls of secrecy surrounding the Bruegel Mystery as well. The others have kept silent long enough for me. It's time to speak out.

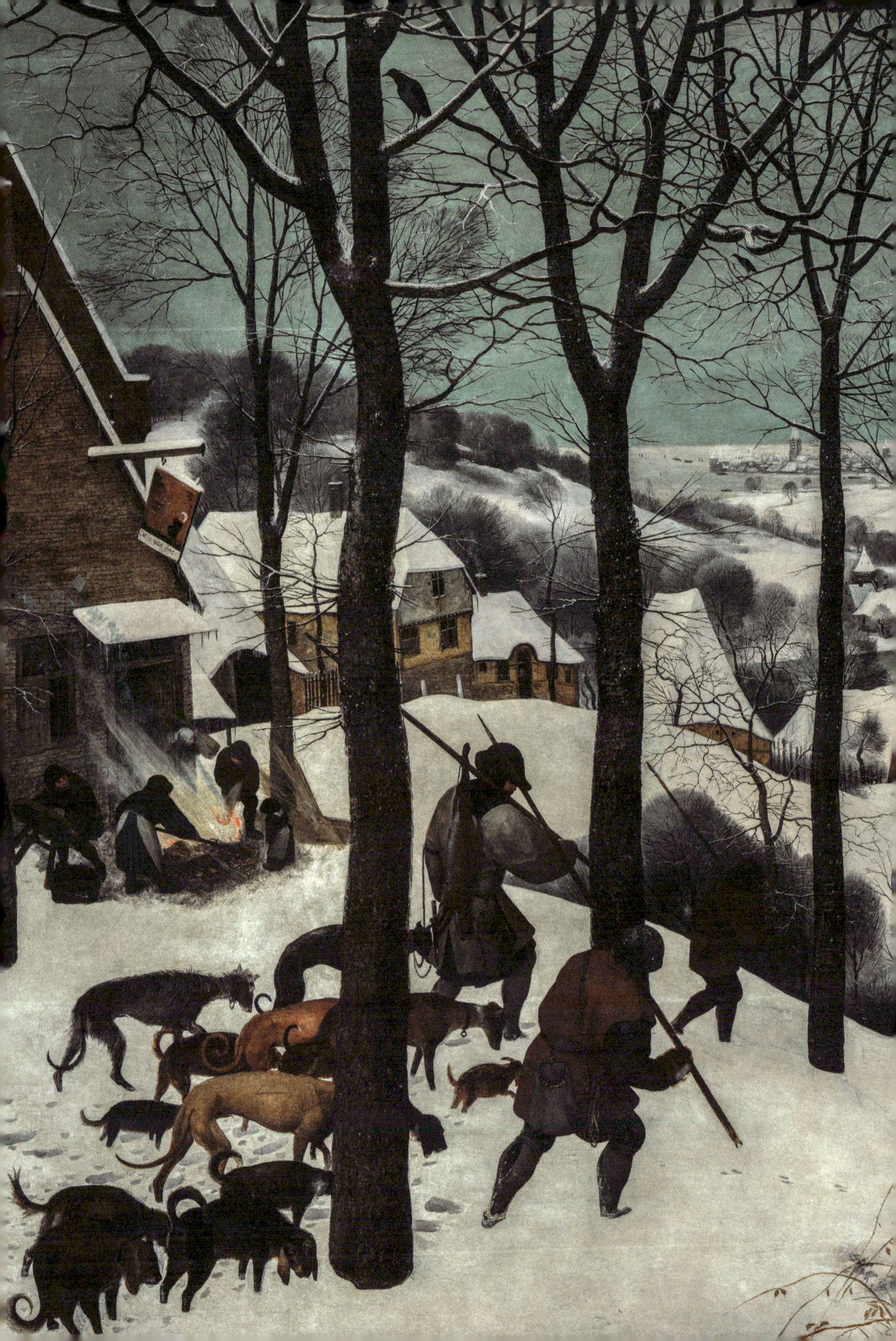

Antwerp, 1989

1. Hunters in the Snow

It all started with the dogs in that magazine which lay open on the recreation room table. They weren't real dogs, I mean, they weren't pictures of dogs, they were in a painting. I didn't give a toss about paintings back then – in fact, I didn't give a toss about anything – but this one I felt strangely attracted to. I slipped the magazine under my sweater to have a closer look at it in bed.

We slept in rooms for two which bordered a wide corridor, I shared mine with Freddy Stadman. The rooms were allocated alphabetically, with Teugels coming after Stadman. But at the time I was convinced they'd saddled me with Freddy to make us the laughing stock of Prince Albert's.

Apart from being a redhead I was quite short for my age. Just how short became painfully clear when I stood next to Stadman. For he was as big and as fat as a bear. Beside this giant panda of a boy I looked like a little koala bear.

From day one the boys called him Fat Freddy and changed his last name from *Stadman* to *Fatman*. They never tired of singing their variation of the Batman tune.

'Deudeu, deudeu, deudeu, deudeu, Fatman! Fatman!'

I heard it a million times outside our bedroom door. But never ever did Freddy storm into the corridor and bang the bullies' heads together, which would have been easy enough with these bear paws of his. In fact, I had to stop myself from doing it in his place. But back then Freddy Stadman and I didn't stand up for each other. We both lived in our own little world and fought a lonely battle.

I guess a tip of the magazine must have shown from under my sweater because suddenly Sebastian grabbed it and ran off with it. Sebastian was the smartest boy in class and wanted to be the best at everything.

'What are you trying to smuggle into your room, Teugels?' he cried.

'Give it back!' I shouted.

He held the magazine in the air where I couldn't reach it. Boys came running out of their rooms to see what was happening.

'Redhead's got dirty pictures,' Jeff exclaimed. He wasn't smart, but he was strong and willing to do anything to win Sebastian's favour.

'Give it back, you bastard!' I tried to bite and kick Sebastian. For if Freddy was a gentle Saint Bernard, I was a biting Pekinese. But Jeff grabbed me and held me.

'Show us! Show us!' the boys shouted as they danced around Sebastian. He held the magazine high above his head, glanced through it and let it fall to the ground. The boys went for it like dogs for a bone. Jeff let go of me. By the time the morons took to their rooms, the magazine was all but ripped to pieces.

Only then did Freddy venture into the corridor. I watched him put the magazine back together as best he could. He handed it to me and I took it without either of us saying a word.

The picture with the dogs was badly wrinkled but not torn. I smoothed it with my hand and let it rest against my knees. In the painting a pack of dogs followed three hunters trudging ankle-deep through the snow. The animals were worn out, hanging their heads. Down in the valley people were skating on the frozen ponds. It must have been cold and yet the whole scene gave me a warm feeling. It reminded me of Christmas at home and long walks in the snow with my dog, Max. Now all I had left of him was the black pebble stone. I called it my dummy-stone, because it gave me comfort, just like a dummy comforts a baby.

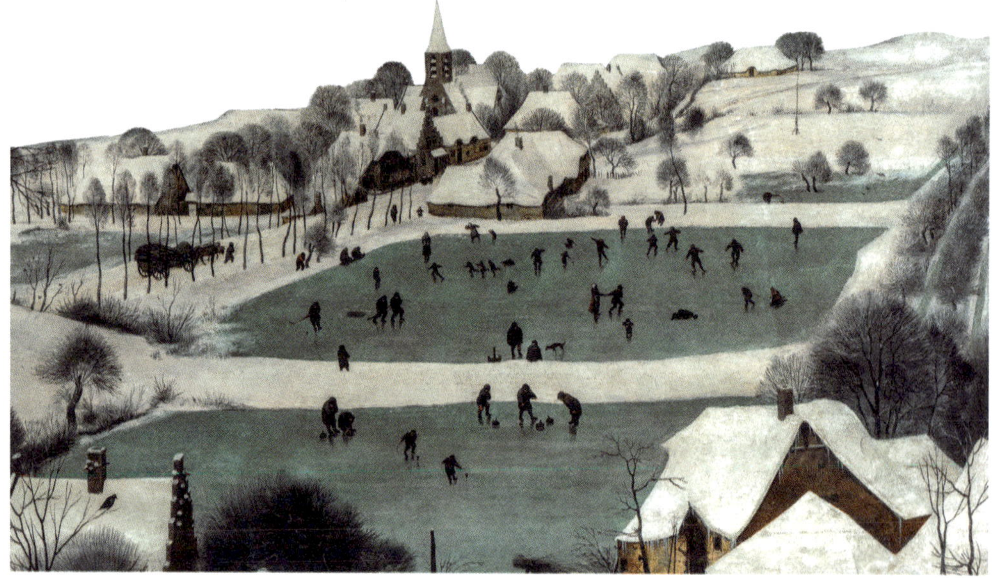

'Bedtime!' De Letter hollered down the corridor, I almost sent the magazine flying. Supervisor De Letter did credit to his name, he knew the school rules backwards and applied them to the letter. I did not know what the penalty was for smuggling magazines to bed, but I bet De Letter did. So I quickly hid the magazine under my mattress.

'I don't want to hear another peep out of you boys.' It was De Letter's way of saying goodnight. As he closed the corridor door, I closed my eyes. Putting my hand on the dummy-stone, as I always did when going to sleep, I saw the painting before me. And I had the strangest sensation I was being sucked into it.

The dogs made soft yapping sounds. I sat on my heels and clicked my tongue the way I used to when I called Max. One of the dogs headed in my direction, wagging its tail. But a single word from one of the hunters made him re-join the pack. That was okay with me, dogs must obey their masters.

I watched the hunters descend the snowy slope towards the village. As the barking and yapping of the dogs faded away, I heard children playing on the ice down in the valley, their happy laughter carrying far in the thin winter air. It seemed like ages since I'd had fun and all of a sudden I felt this urge to join them. So, I took off in the hunters' tracks. They led me deeper and deeper into the wood until all I heard was the snow crunching beneath my feet. I stopped and listened. All was silent and white. A crow cried, three times. For some reason that sent shivers down my spine and I moved on. As the wood started to clear rooftops came into view. The children's voices resounded once again, only this time the laughter was replaced by cries of fear. Another sharp cry, not a crow this time, it was a woman shrieking, something must have happened. Maybe someone fell through the ice. I hurried down the steep slope. A final bend and suddenly I found myself on the edge of the village square full of people running and screaming. It took me a while to grasp what I was witnessing.

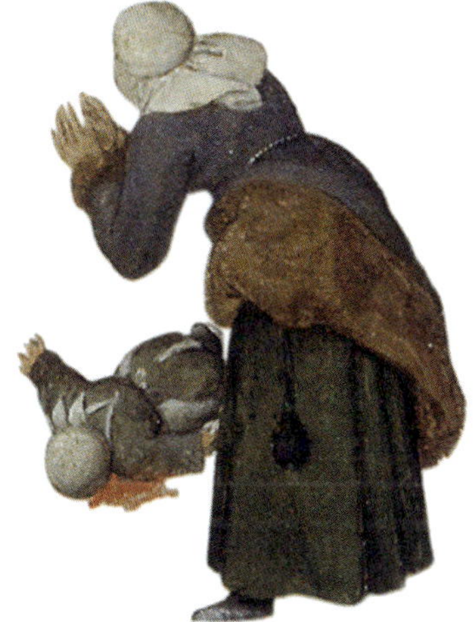

'I beg you, please!' a woman's voice cried out right beside me. 'Spare my child!' I turned and saw a young mother pressing her baby against her breast. A brute grabbed the child by its legs and hit the woman hard in the face. For a split second she loosened her grip but that was enough for him to tear the baby from her arms. I couldn't believe what

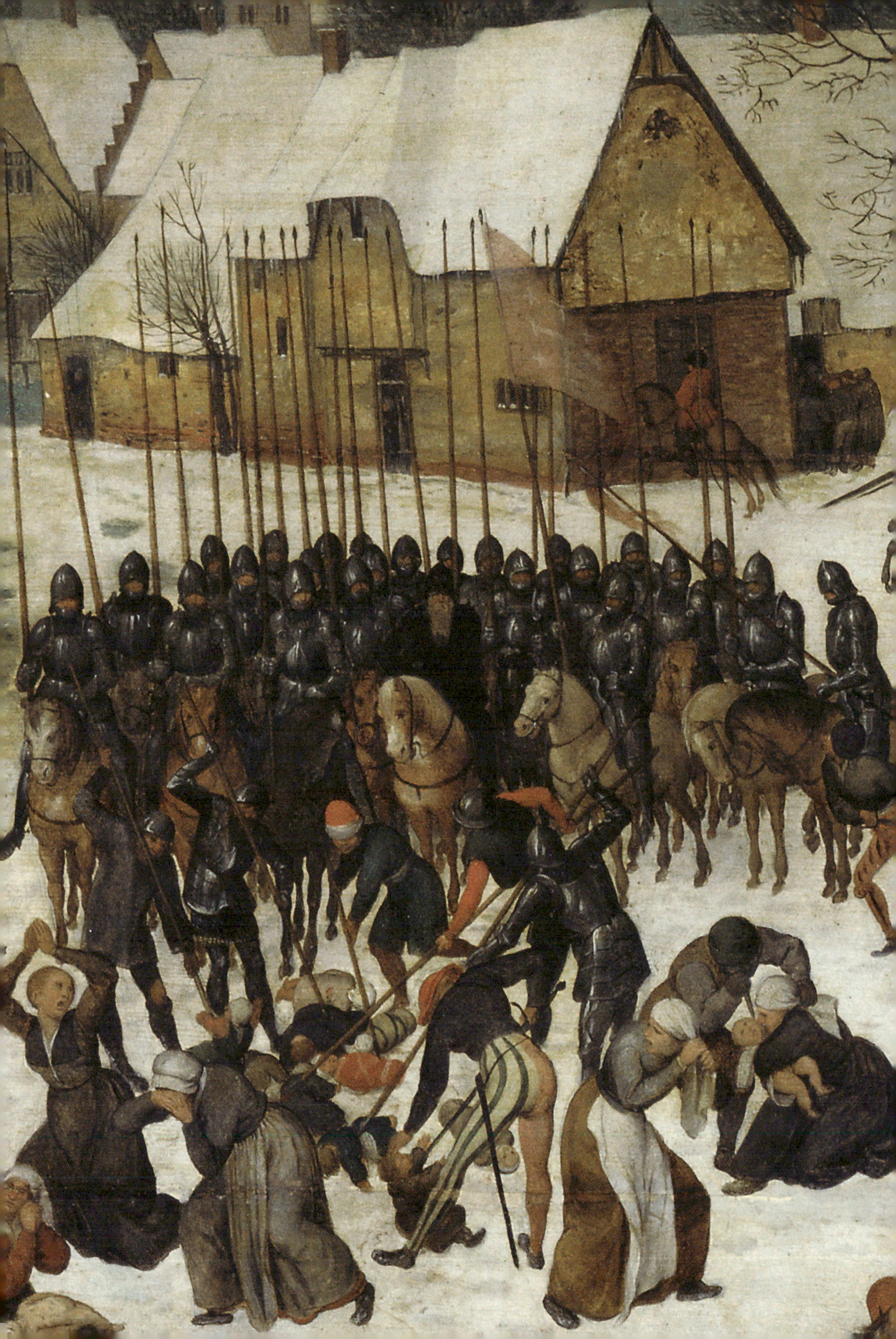

happened next. The brute threw the baby on the ground and pierced it with a sword. I watched in horror as the snow around the little body turned red.

The square was crawling with armed men. They broke down doors and dragged children out, their parents hanging onto them for dear life. A mother was pulling her hair, insane with grief. A father fell to his knees, begging. But the brutes were merciless and slit the children's throats or set dogs loose on them.

What had I stumbled into? Was this a dream or was it really happening? On the far side of the square was a group of armoured soldiers on horseback. How could they just sit and watch this massacre? Why didn't they stop this madness? Or were they to make sure no child escaped?

Suddenly one of the horsemen caught sight of me. Even over that distance I felt his eyes burning into mine. With a sudden motion he pulled the reins of his horse. The next instant I was running up the road leading out of the village. Soon the shrieking grew fainter, it must have been the snow, muffling all sounds. I stopped to catch my breath. The silence was deathly.

The moment I heard the dull thud of hooves, I knew it was too late to hide. The soldier had already seen me and reined in his horse. Clouds of white steam spewed from its nostrils. I turned and fled up the slippery path, but behind me the hooves were rapidly closing in on me. I slipped and fell. The horseman's spurs jangled as he jumped to the ground. There was the bloodcurdling sound of metal upon metal as he drew his sword from its scabbard. Zingggg. I saw him raise his sword to chop my head off, when suddenly out of nowhere a dog jumped up and sunk his teeth into his arm. Crying out in pain he dropped his sword...

A split second later I found myself back in bed.

'Teugels, wake up!' a voice whispered urgently. 'Wake up, Ben!'

It took me a few moments to realize it was Freddy Stadman who had me by the collar and was shaking me awake. All of a sudden, he let go of me, his bed creaked as he threw himself in. I heard De Letter walking down the corridor, stopping outside our room he sniffed the air as if he smelt a rat. As I held my breath, I had a flashback of the dog appearing out of nowhere. Was it my imagination or did it really have a white spot on its chest?

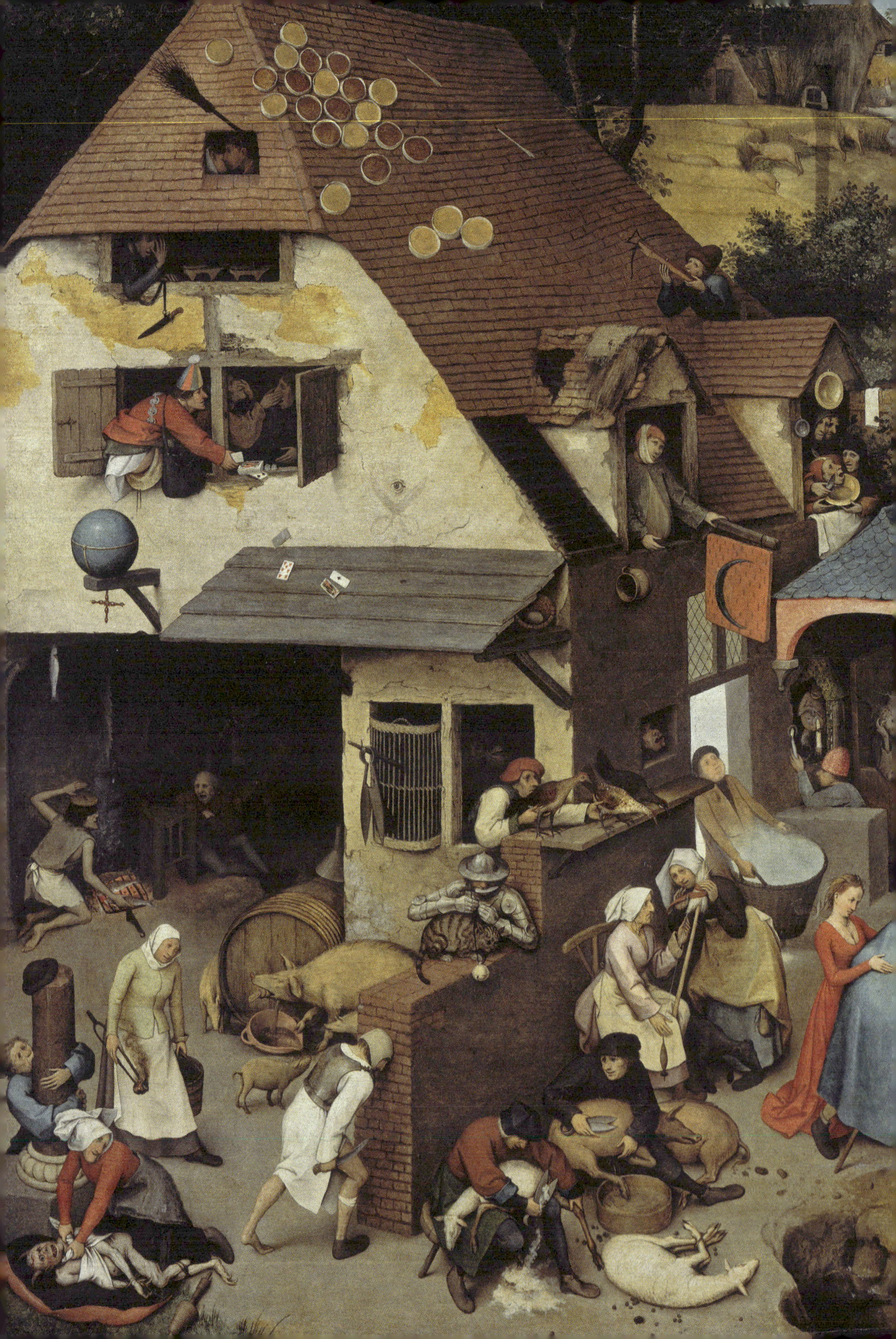

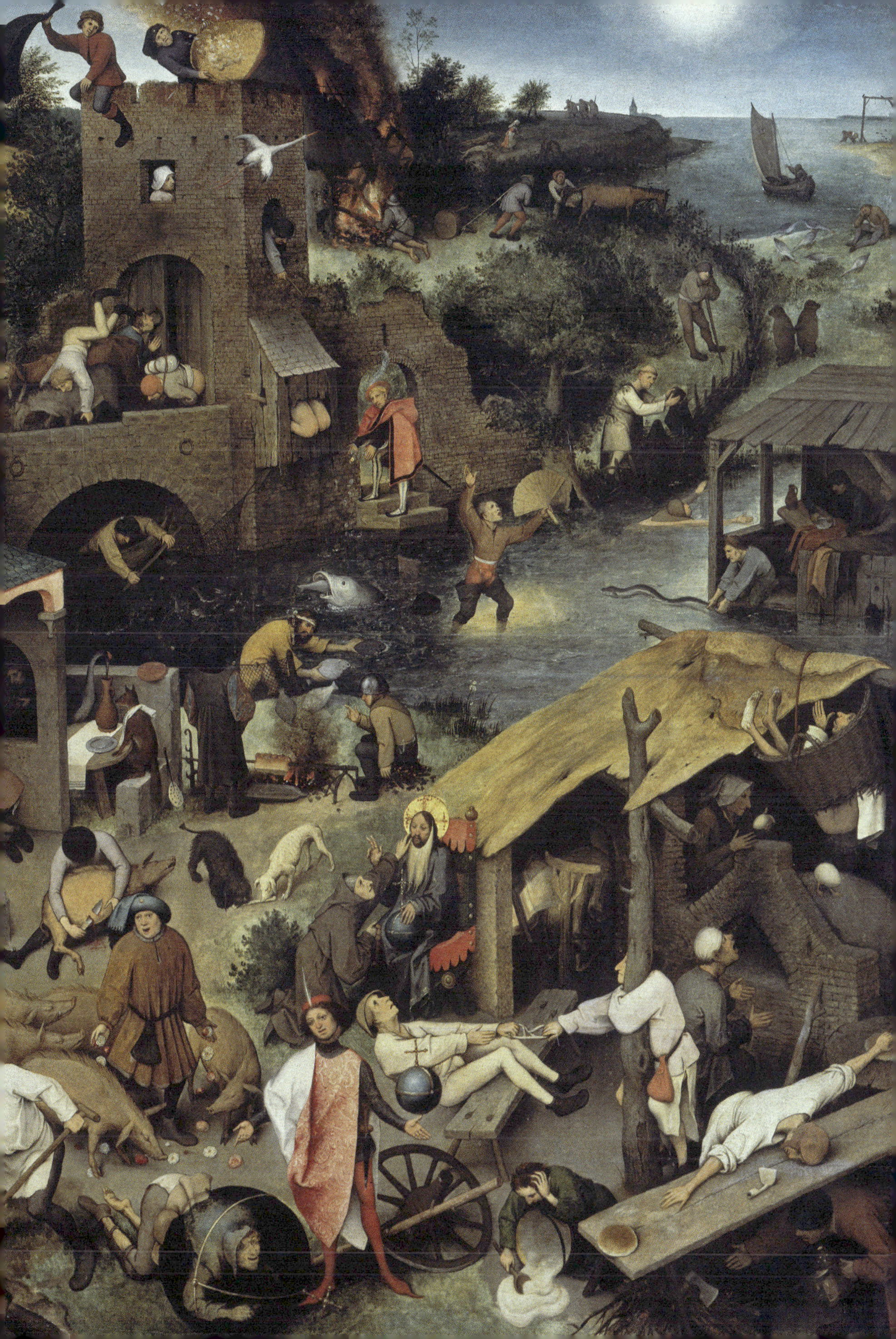

2. The Proverbs

The moment he heard children's voices shattering the sacred silence of the Antwerp Royal Museum of Fine Arts, Pieter Douwe was on his guard.

'Keep it down, boys! This is a museum, not a playground.' Douwe recognized the voice of Miss Vriends. She was a Dutch teacher at Prince Albert's boarding school for boys and every year took her first-year pupils to see Bruegel's *Proverbs*. School visits, Pieter Douwe knew after forty-one years as a museum attendant, required extra vigilance, because children couldn't keep their hands to themselves. And woe betide anyone who dared so much as point a finger at his Bruegels. Having watched over them for over four decades, that's how he had come to regard the paintings, they were his, his to protect.

So he kept a sharp look-out as Miss Vriends led her class into the Bruegel hall. He nodded a greeting to her and she nodded back. She was a middle-aged woman, warm and caring by the looks of her, who knew how to handle youngsters.

'Okay, boys,' she said, 'all the paintings in this hall are by Pieter Bruegel, perhaps the greatest painter of his time.'

'Perhaps?' Douwe wanted to cry out. 'Bruegel is the best ever!'

One of the boys put his hand up.

'Yes, Jeff? What is it?'

'Can I ask a question, Miss?'

'Well, what do you know, Jeff showing some interest. Okay, ask away.'

'I wonder,' the boy said innocently, 'did Bruegel have red hair?'

'Red hair?' Miss Vriends said, puzzled. 'Whatever gave you that idea?'

'Well, it's just that Bruegel sounds so much like Teugels.'

The whole class burst out laughing and looked at a boy standing to the side. He was small and had flaming red hair. Next to him was a big boy, who didn't join in the laughter.

'That's enough!' Vriends said angrily. 'Jeff, if you think you're being funny, you are badly mistaken. Stop being such a child, you hear?' Then she turned to the boy with the red hair. 'Ben, can you remind class which painting in particular we've come here to see?'

The boy didn't reply, not even after the big boy had bent over and whispered something into his ear.

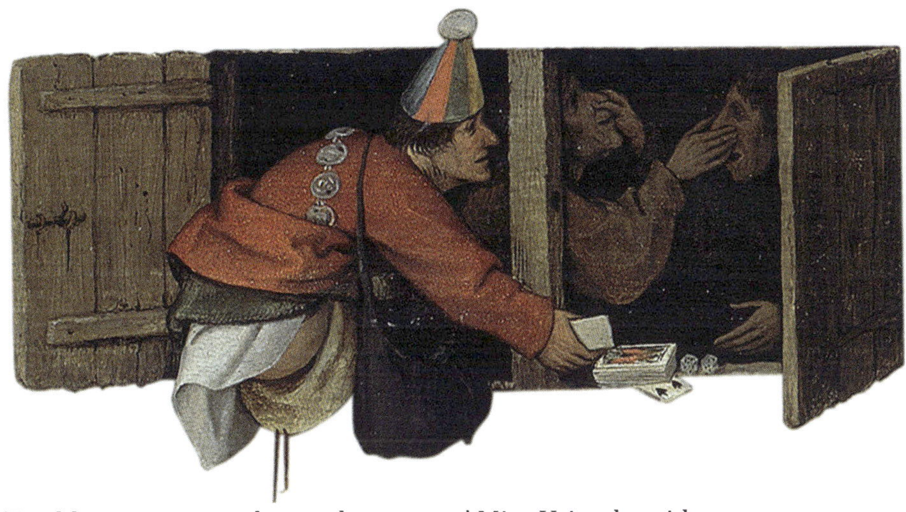

'Freddy, you seem to know the answer,' Miss Vriends said.

'*The proverbs*, miss,' the boy said.

'That's right. We learnt some proverbs in class. Now let's go and see whether we can point any of them out in the actual painting. Follow me.'

I know all the proverbs by heart, Douwe thought. I can point them out blindfolded. From time to time, when there were no visitors, he'd play this little game. He'd close his eyes, think of a proverb, *to crap on the world* for example, and put his finger down. Not on the actual painting, of course, but on the reference scheme beside it. And there he was, upper left, a man in a red coat sticking his arse out of the window, crapping on the globe beneath him. In the next window two men were leading each other by the nose. There were lots of proverbs referring to parts of the body. *To bang one's head against a brick wall*, for instance. Or *to look through one's fingers, to keep one's eye on the sail*...

Keeping his eye on the visitors, that's what he should be doing, Douwe suddenly realized, rather than just stand there daydreaming. He rushed over to Miss Vriends and her class.

'Right. And then we come to the proverbs with animals,' Miss Vriends said. 'Who can point one out with an animal?'

There's lots of them, Douwe thought. *To bell the cat, to try to kill two flies with one stroke, the big fish eat the small ones, two dogs fighting over a bone*... In fact, there wasn't a painting in the hall that still held secrets for him. After forty-odd years he knew every little figure Bruegel had painted, their postures, their expressions, how they were dressed. Every tree, cart, animal or beer jug he'd studied endlessly. At times he was so consumed by the paintings, he thought he could hear the laughter at *The Peasant Wedding* or the shrieks at *The Massacre of the Innocents*.

Douwe often thought about the paintings as windows on Bruegel's world. If only he could find the key.

'Keep up, boys!' Miss Vriends said as she ushered her pupils out. Once again, Douwe realized, his mind had wandered. Was he getting too old for the job? He was over sixty and started to feel his age. His knees ached and from time to time he felt a strange kind of pressure on his chest. And so ever more often he sneaked off to a little storage room at the back of the museum and took a nap on a discarded sofa.

As the last boys left the hall, Miss Vriends nodded goodbye. Douwe gave her a smile. He was glad to have his Bruegels all to himself again. With a sigh of relief, he looked around the room and gave a start. There was still someone there, it was the boy with the red hair. He just stood there, like a statue, staring at one of Bruegel's more gruesome paintings, *The Massacre of the Innocents*.

'You there. Keep your distance,' Douwe called out to the boy just as Miss Vriends came rushing back in.

'Ah, there you are!' she said relieved, but the boy didn't react. It wasn't until Miss Vriends took him by the shoulders, that he seemed to awaken. 'Are you all right, Ben?' she asked as she led him away.

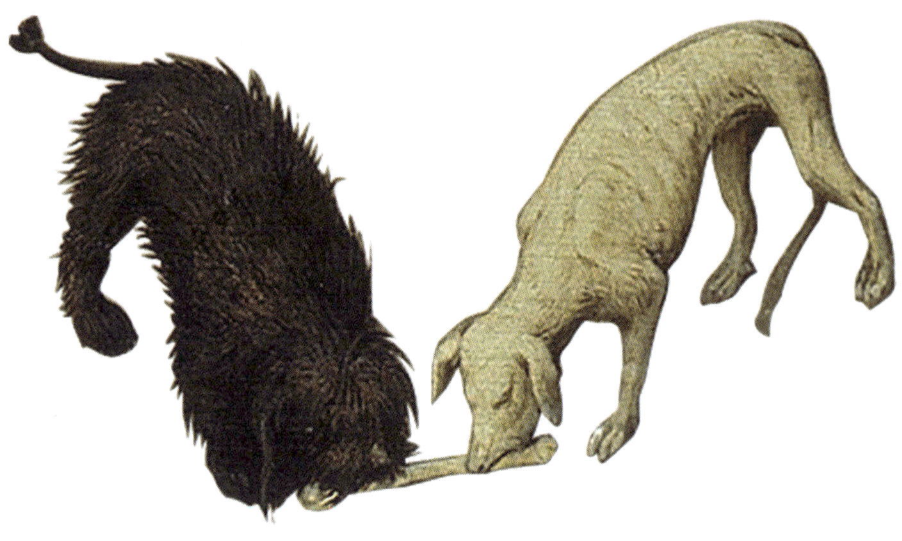

3. More than a dream

For days on end I racked my brains, trying to figure out how my nightmare could turn up in that museum? We were walking past it as Miss Vriends showed us the way to *The Proverbs*. I stopped dead in my tracks, recognizing the village square at a glance. In the painting nothing moved. But in my mind's eye the whole dreadful scene came back to life. Only the horsemen stood still and watched. Where was the one who had almost chopped my head off? There! There he was. My heart missed a beat when I noticed he was looking straight at me, through the paint, the canvas and the centuries. 'I'll get you. You'll see,' his grin said. Fear gripped me by the throat, I wanted to get away from that painting, away from that murderer, but I couldn't move. Luckily miss Vriends broke the spell.

I had to talk it over with someone before my head burst. But who with? The first person I thought of was Vriends, my favourite teacher by far. But did I want to make an eternal fool of myself by dishing up such a half-baked story? No, Vriends was out. Then who? Another teacher? Not in a thousand years. A classmate? I'd just as soon bite off my tongue.

And then, out of the blue, the occasion presented itself. Or should I say out of the grey? Because it was heavily overcast when Dhondt, our gym teacher, led us out onto the football field. Dhondt was nicknamed Boxer because he had the flat face of a Boxer-dog. Come rain or shine, Boxer had us play our weekly football match. He kept count of the scores and at the end of the schoolyear he awarded a Most Valuable Player trophy.

I hated these matches, but worse still was the preceding humiliating ritual of team formation. Sebastian, on top of being the smartest boy in class, was the best at sports too. Sebèstian the boys called him behind his back, no need to say he was Boxer's favourite.

'Right, Sebastian,' Boxer yelled every so often, 'you show these lot how a real sportsman goes about this.' The smirk on Sebastian's face as he did so, turned my stomach. It goes without saying that Sebastian got first pick at team formation. As a rule, Sebastian was captain of the A team and most of the time Jeff led the B team. Picture us on the muddy field, shivering in our silly outfits. Sebastian and Jeff selected the better players and then the reasonable ones, until all that was left was a bunch of losers nobody wanted in their team and who stood there pretending nothing was amiss. Needless to say, Freddy and I always ended up in that group.

This time, his patience wearing thin, Boxer decided himself.

'Teugels and Stadman, you're with Jeff. The other two with Sebastian. Come on, let's get started.'

Jeff had made me last defender and Freddy goalkeeper. I guess he reckoned the rest of them would keep the other team away from our goal. At first this seemed to work. If I wasn't mistaken our team had already scored. But I had other things on my mind. A few feet away Freddy stood gazing at the dark clouds as if he was weighing the chances of it beginning to pour.

'I say, Stadman,' I said tentatively, 'thanks for waking me up the other night, when I had this nightmare.'

'Don't mention it,' he said. That seemed to settle the matter for him because he shifted his attention to the clouds again. But I wanted him to pay attention to me. 'I know it sounds incredible,' I said, 'but I saw my dream in the museum the other day.' This time Freddy looked straight at me. Knowing he was all ears now, it was as if a dam broke and it all came gushing out.

'My dream wasn't just a dream, I mean, it's also a painting...by Bruegel. You know, the painter we went to the museum for. *The Massacre of the Innocents* is what it's called. That's what it said on the nameplate. I swear I had never laid eyes on it before in my life. Never, Stadman. And yet I saw it all happen in my dream and I was right there in the middle of it. It was so real, so...'

I fell silent, lost for words while Freddy just kept looking at me. He thinks I've gone mad, is what I thought. Actually, he was wondering whether I wasn't pulling his leg, but decided then and there to trust me and asked a very intelligent question.

'Was that other work by Bruegel too?'

My immediate reaction was 'What a silly question, of course it was! All the paintings in that hall were by Bruegel.' For some reason I assumed that fat people were automatically thick in the head as well. But I was about to find out just how smart Freddy Stadman was.

'I'm not talking about the museum,' he said patiently. 'I'm talking about the picture in the magazine you smuggled into our room. The one with the dogs in the snow. Was that a Bruegel too?'

'Teugels! Where's your defence?' Boxer hollered.

I'd completely forgotten about the match and hadn't seen the ball coming. I made a half-hearted attempt to stop it, but Sebastian was quicker. He dribbled the ball round me and scored. Freddy hadn't moved an inch.

'Stadman,' Boxer yelled, 'are you a goal-keeper or a goal-sleeper?' All the boys but Jeff laughed their heads off at his lame joke. 'And you, Teugels, you have to block your opponent.' He took the ball and held it right in front of my nose. 'This, Teugels,' he said as if it was a wisdom, 'is *your* ball, you hear? Your ball!' Then he headed for centre spot.

'You'll never play in my team again, you fat-ass,' Jeff snapped. 'Neither will you, red midget!'

All of a sudden it started to pour but there was no way Boxer was going to suspend the match. Meanwhile Sebastian had got possession of the ball and headed straight for our goal.

'Okay, Ben,' I said to myself, 'it's your ball.' I slid towards the ball, knocking Sebastian off his feet.

Boxer blew his whistle and pointed to the penalty mark. 'That was a dirty tackle, Teugels,' he cried as he gave me a red card. 'But it's better than doing nothing,' he added softly.

Sebastian, who had been nursing a painful ankle, prepared to take the penalty shot with streaks of mud running down his face.

'Remember what I said, Stadman,' Boxer shouted. 'Move!'

Freddy did as he was told. Like a red Indian dancing around a fire he started hopping from one foot to the other while under his rain-soaked T-shirt rolls of fat danced along. Boxer gave the signal and as Sebastian ran up to kick the ball, Freddy suddenly dropped the Indian act and started waving his arms like a runaway windmill. Was Sebastian distracted or did he have dirt in his eyes, the fact is his shot sailed way over.

For a while all you could hear was the heavy rain pounding on the muddy field.

'Sebastian, how on earth could you miss?' Boxer yelled. 'That'll cost you in the ranking for Most Valuable Player.'

I, on the other hand, got my first and only point ever from Boxer.

4. A Book on Bruegel

'Ben?' Miss Vriends said as I entered the school library. 'What a surprise to see you here.'

In fact, I could hardly believe it myself. Me being in the library, I mean. But this was an emergency.

'I'd like a book on Bruegel, please Miss', I said nervously. 'One with pictures of all his paintings.'

'Well, well. I do believe our little outing to the museum bore some fruit after all. You just wait here, Ben, and I'll see what I can dig up for you.' She disappeared between the bookshelves.

I looked around nervously, hoping she'd be quick about it. I didn't want any of the boys to see me here and start sticking their noses into my secret.

Miss Vriends returned with two books, one large and one small. 'Now this one', she said opening the large book, 'you have to be extra careful with.' It contained full-page colour pictures on shiny paper and must have weighed a ton.

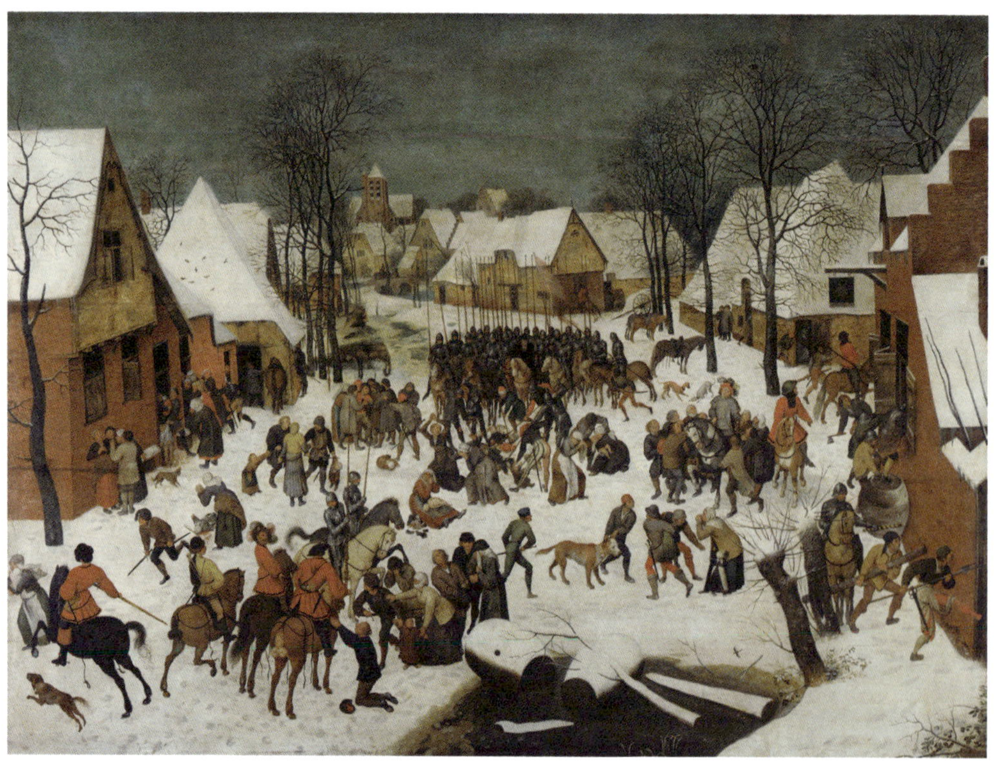

'I'll take the small book', I said. That one was so much easier to hide.

'All right, let me just fill out your card.' While she was writing, she gave me a furtive look, both amused and inquisitive. 'There you are', she said handing me the book.

'Thanks, Miss.' I ran outside, glad she hadn't asked any questions. In a quiet corner I leafed through the book. It didn't take me long to find what I was looking for: *Massacre of the Innocents*, my nightmare. And sure enough, a few pages further on was the painting with the dogs. It was called *Hunters in the snow*.

In the recreation room that evening Freddy and I hunched over the Bruegel book like two conspirators. We got some sideways glances from the other boys, but they left us in peace.

'So now we know for certain they're both Bruegels', I whispered excitedly.

'Yes, but not just any Bruegels,' Freddy said as he turned from one picture to the other. 'Both of them are winter scenes.'

'So? Does that make any difference?'

'Of course it does. It means you're not confined to the painting you land in, you

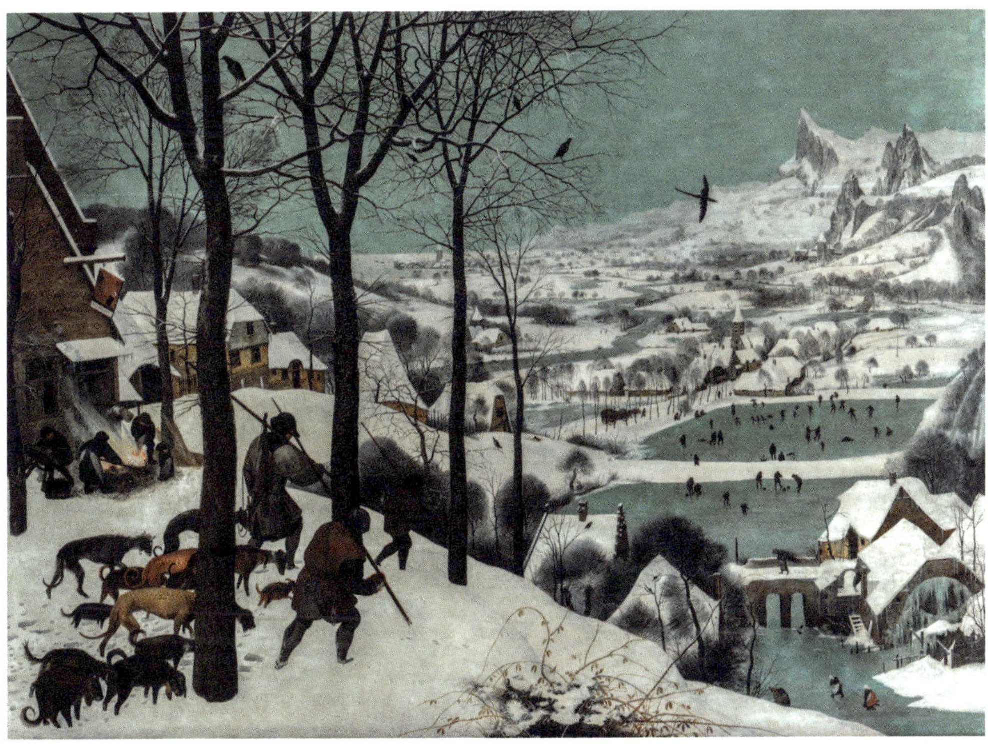

can wander round Bruegel's world. And this time it was winter there.'

There was only one way to find out if Freddy's theory was correct. I had to try and get into another Bruegel.

'But no more winter scenes,' I said. 'I don't want to bump into that murdering horseman again.'

'I'll find you a good painting,' Freddy said. As he leafed through the book, I saw cripples, blindmen, walking skeletons, weird creatures half man half animal. And each time I quickly looked away for fear of ending up in one of them. That Bruegel fellow sure had a twisted imagination.

Eventually we chose *The Peasant Wedding*. Surely nothing bad could happen to me there. It all looked peaceful enough, with people eating and drinking to the sound of bagpipes.

'That pie looks delicious,' Freddy said pointing at the tray of plates.

'That dog looks very much like Max,' I said pointing at the dog under the table. We were so caught up in the book we hadn't noticed Sebastian coming up to us.

'Don't you try that trick on me again, Fat Freddy!' he said pointing a threatening finger. 'You made me miss my penalty shot with your silly moves. But I won't have anyone stealing points from me, you hear!'

5. Peasant Wedding

'Ben?' Freddy whispered.

I was thinking of Sebastian. What made him so terribly ambitious? Why did he have to be the best at everything?

'Ben?' Freddy again.

'Yes, Freddy, what's the matter?' Somewhere along the way we had started to call each other by our first name.

'O, you're still awake,' Freddy said. 'I was just wondering if you were already there.'

'Where?'

'At the wedding, of course.'

The Bruegel book lay open at the picture of The Peasant Wedding.

'How can I get there if you keep me awake?'

'Okay, okay. I'll keep quiet.'

I put my hand on the dummy-stone and my eyelids grew heavy.

The painting exploded into life, the bagpipes almost drowned by the hubbub in the barn. At the long table people were eating and drinking away. Two men carried

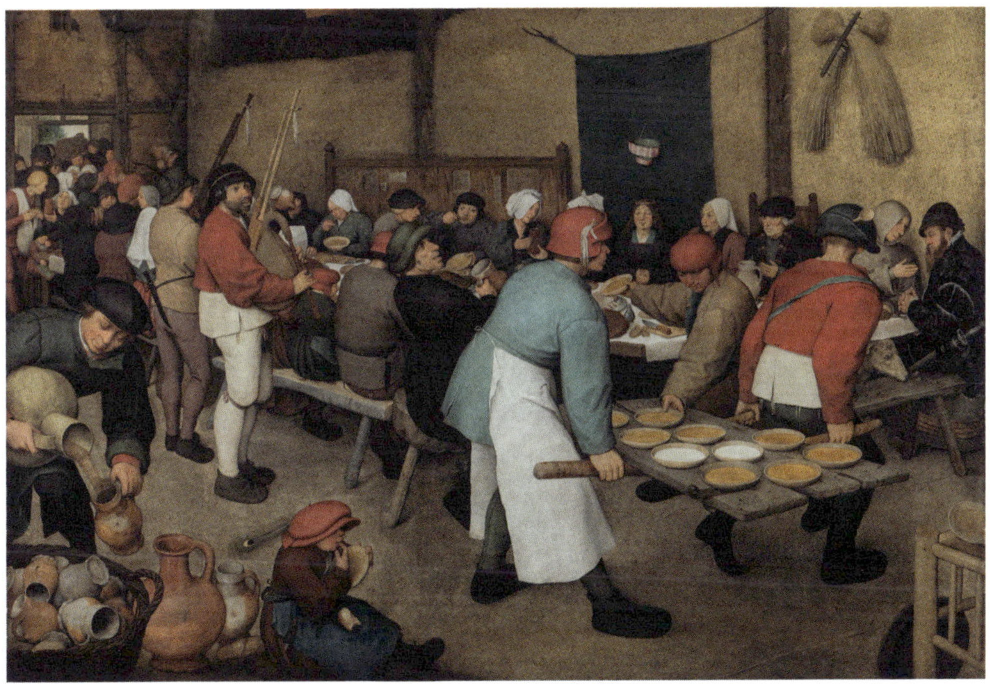

plates of pie on a large tray, which was actually a door on two poles. Another man was taking jugs from a wicker basket and filled them with beer.

No-one seemed to have noticed my sudden appearance. Not even the child with the red hat right next to me, that was eating pie with its fingers. Only the dog under the table had seen me straight away, it was at the feet of a gentleman dressed in black, who was listening to a monk. Now that I saw the dog in real life the resemblance with Max was even more striking: reddish fur, black snout, but no white spot on its chest.

I clicked my tongue and the dog came out from under the table. This time the man in black had seen me too. As I crouched down and put out my hand, the dog came towards me, wagging its tail. The man smiled at me and resumed his conversation with the monk. It felt good to touch a dog again. Stroking its neck I noticed its collar. To my great surprise it was the same as Max's: a pebble stone on a strap. Only, this one was grey and said Rex.

'Rex?' I said and he circled round me. I suddenly realized how much I'd missed a dog's company. The gate at the other side of the barn stood wide open. I pushed my way through the crowd and Rex followed. Outside peasants and their wives were dancing to a bagpiper's tunes, their hopping got the dog all excited.

'Here, Rex.' Clapping my hand against my thigh I led the dog away from the commotion. Once we reached the fields outside the village, where the corn was ripe, I let the dog run loose. He raced way ahead of me, came running back, circled my legs and shot off again. I stopped and closed my eyes, listening to the sound of birds and insects in the warm summer air.

Zingggg! The silence was shattered by a sound that sent shivers down my spine. The sound of metal upon metal, the horseman pulling his sword from its scabbard. How had he found me? This time it wasn't winter, it was high summer. I dove into a ditch and bit my lip to keep from crying out in fear. My heart missed a beat when Rex jumped on top of me. I held him tightly.

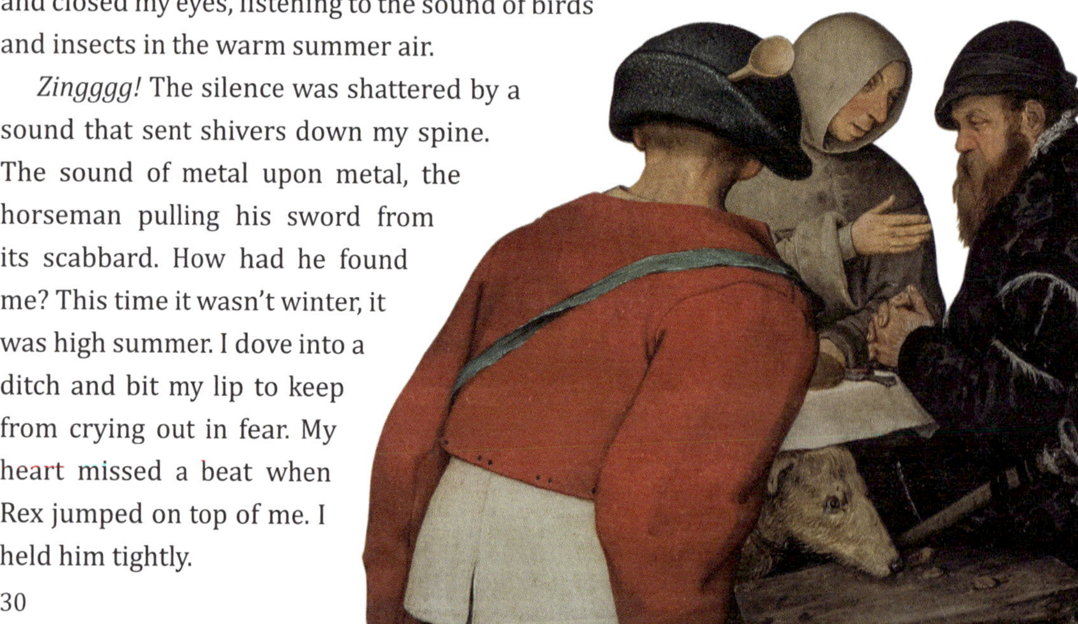

Zingggg. Zingggg. O help! There were two of them out there. Before I could stop him Rex ran into the cornfield, barking. Any minute now they'd cut him down. But Rex just kept on barking a few yards from where I was crouching.

'Quiet', a woman's voice said. As the dog stopped barking, I could hear muffled laughter. That didn't sound like people were being massacred. I summoned all my courage and crawled into the corn field on all fours. I came upon an open space where the corn had already been cut. In the shade of a tree a group of women were having a meal while a peasant was taking a nap.

Zinggggg came the sound to the left of me. Ever so carefully I stuck my head out. There was a peasant, holding a scythe upside down. He ran a whetstone over the blade. *Zingggg* sang the scythe.

The sun was setting by the time Rex and I returned to the village. Outside the barn people were still dancing and drinking. I was dying with thirst. There was a jug on the table behind the bagpiper's back, I took it and put it to my mouth. The beer was lukewarm but I drank it thirstily. Just as I entered the barn they brought in a new load of pie. My stomach grumbled. I put the empty jug in the wicker basket and took a plate off the tray. And while Rex drank the water the gentleman in black had given him, I started scooping the pie with my fingers.

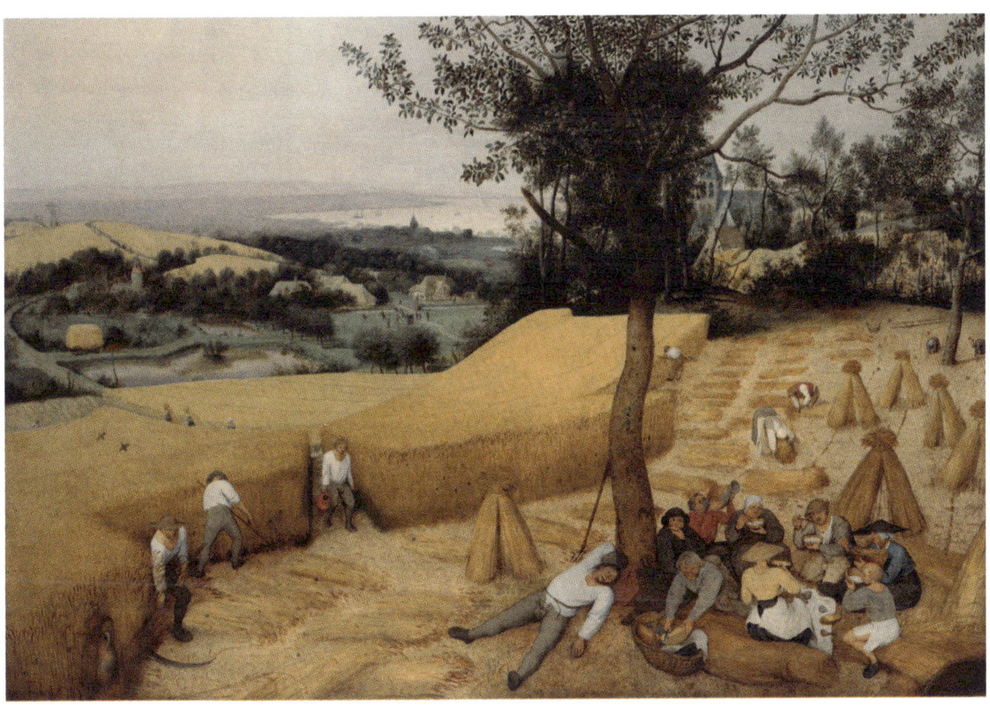

'And then this here gentleman felt he had to bring me back,' I said teasing Freddy.

It was Wednesday, we had the afternoon off and had decided to spend it in the park, where the lilacs were in bloom.

'I was worried,' Freddy defended himself. 'I thought you were drowning the way you kept on swallowing.'

'Of course I was swallowing,' I cried. 'I was eating the best pie I ever ate.'

'So that's why you kept licking your fingers.'

'You should have tasted that pie, Freddy.'

'You know what? Next time you let me lick your fingers.'

We both laughed out loud. It felt good to be laughing again. Then we walked on, lost in thought. It realized I hadn't been this happy in a long, long time. I could tell from the way he walked that Freddy was happy too.

'It's a good thing that I have you, Freddy,' I said. 'Otherwise I might still be stuck in that barn.'

'The mechanics of your Bruegel trips are a complete riddle to me.'

I stopped and got my dummy-stone from under my T-shirt. 'I've been thinking this may have something to do with it.'

'What is that?' Freddy said as he turned the pebble stone this way and that.

'My dog's tag.'

'You have a dog?'

'I used to. His name was Max. I got him from my parents when I turned six.'

'So what happened?'

'Max got hit by a car. My parents too were killed in a car accident.'

Freddy put his warm bear paws on my shoulders. 'I'm really sorry for you, Little Red Riding Hood.' It didn't sound like a nickname at all coming from his mouth. I felt the weight of his hands and yet it was as if a load was lifted from my shoulders, I no longer felt utterly alone.

'So what makes you think this little stone has anything to do with it?' Freddy asked after a while.

'Because the dog in *The Peasant Wedding* wears one just like it. His one says Rex but it's got the same numbers on it: one, five, five, seven. I think that must be the year 1557.'

'Wow, talking about coincidences! But however did you come by it?'

'I found it in my aunt Jo's attic. She's my guardian.'

'You don't seem very fond of her. Is she the one who sent you here?'

'That's right. And who sent you?'

'My parents.'

'Your parents? Did they want to be rid of you too?'

'No, they just think I'm too fat.'

'Too fat? You? Don't make me laugh. Whatever gave them that idea?

'They hope a stiff boarding school will work wonders.'

'Well,' I said, 'Prince Albert's already done wonders. Little Red Hiding Hood has found herself a great big teddybear. A Freddybear.'

We fell over laughing. I closed my eyes and felt the sun on my face.

6. The Bruegel Mystery

Pieter Douwe thought he was dreaming. It was still early, an hour before the museum opened its doors, maybe he wasn't quite awake. He rubbed his eyes and counted again, carefully. No, he wasn't mistaken, there was one missing.

'Gone!' he said out loud. 'Vanished! I have to go and tell Bosman.' And he rushed to the director's office as fast as his old legs could carry him.

'Can't you knock, Douwe?' Bosman grumbled as Pieter charged into his office. But the old attendant didn't reply, he just stood there gasping for breath. He made the oddest gestures and looked like he'd just seen the devil in person.

'Come!' was all Douwe was able to utter. And without another word he ran out of the office. Normally the director would not have obeyed such a blunt command, certainly not coming from a subordinate. But seeing how agitated the old man was, he quickly followed him.

'Douwe, what's the matter?' the director called out. His voice rang through the empty museum. 'Douwe, will you just hold on for a second and tell me what's the matter.' But Pieter was already at the other end of the hall and kept running. At the far end of the second hall Bosman caught up with him. 'Will you just... tell me... what's the matter?' he panted as they crossed the third hall side by side.

'Bruegel', Pieter puffed.

I could have guessed, Bosman thought. His bloody Bruegels again.

'Peasant... Wedding', Pieter added.

'What about it?' the director asked, suddenly apprehensive the painting might be damaged. Or even worse, stolen!

As they turned into the Bruegel hall Pieter pointed to the left wall. To Bosman's relief *The Peasant Wedding* was still there. They halted in front of it.

'I don't see... anything... wrong with it', the director panted while he scanned the painting.

Still unable to speak Pieter pointed a trembling finger at the right bottom corner.

'What?' Bosman snapped impatiently. He looked hard at the area Pieter was pointing out: the tray with the plates of pie that were being handed out to the wedding guests.

'Plate missing', the old man said barely audible.

'What?!'

'There's a plate... gone missing...This here plate... is gone.'

'Which plate? There is no plate!'

'Of course there isn't... Because it's gone!'

This time Old Pete's really gone off his rockers, Bosman thought.

'There have always been... ten plates on that tray,' Pieter explained. 'Last night... as I went home... there were ten... now how many are there?'

Like a first former the director pointed out the plates one by one as he counted. 'One, two, three, four, five, six, seven, eight, nine...'

'That's right, nine!' Pieter said, who had regained his wind. 'And right here was plate number ten. Now it's gone.'

'But that's impossible!' the director cried, his voice cracking. 'Things don't just... disappear from paintings!'

'If you don't believe me, go and fetch a reproduction', Pieter said.

At noon Bosman called a press conference in the Bruegel hall. He stood in front of *The Peasant Wedding*, almost hiding the painting from the dozens of reporters, cameramen and photographers. On either side of him were five museum attendants. Douwe kept to the back of the hall.

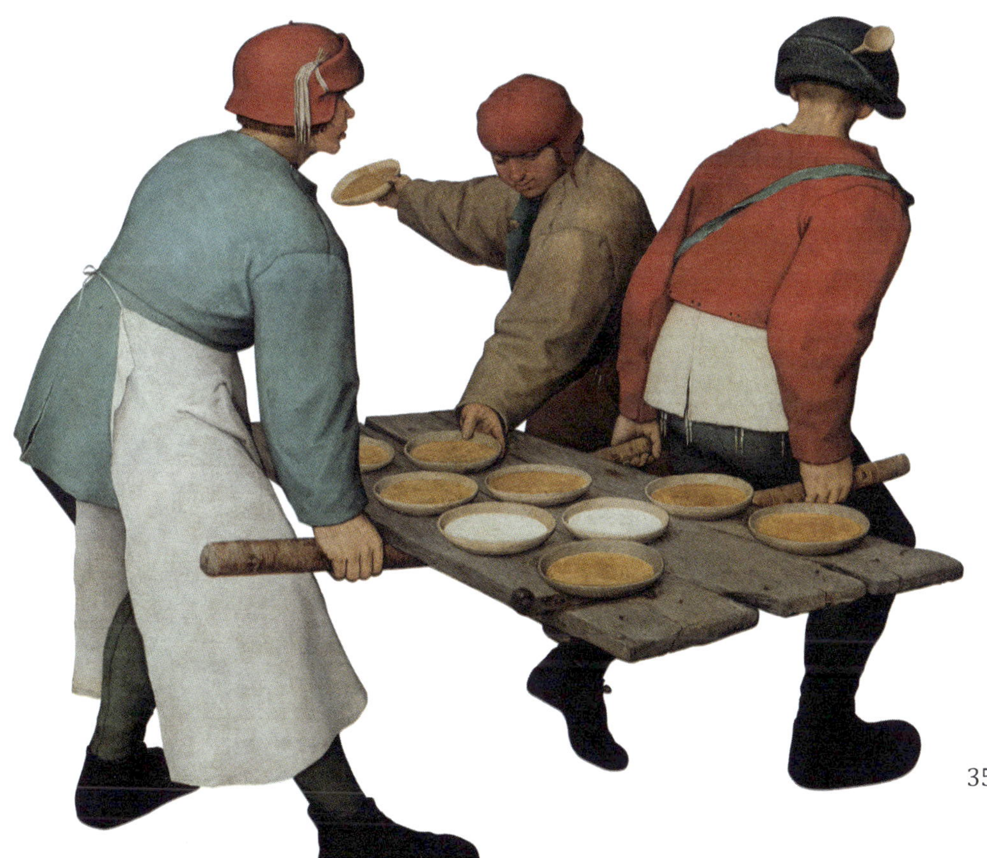

'Ladies and gentlemen,' Bosman said gravely, 'today our museum made a spectacular discovery. It concerns the painting behind me, one of our most prized possessions: *The Peasant Wedding* by the Flemish master Pieter Bruegel the Elder.'

The press people craned their necks trying to catch a glimpse of the painting. 'But first I want to show you a *reproduction* of the painting. You'll understand why in a minute.'

Cameras flashed and lenses zoomed in as two of the attendants held up a large poster.

'Right here is the area that concerns us,' the director said making a circular movement over the large tray. 'As you can see there are ten plates on the tray.' He paused so people were able to count the plates. He then thanked the attendants, who rolled up the poster.

'Now take a look at the original painting.' Theatrically Bosman stepped aside. There was a moment of total silence while people counted.

'Nine', a woman said in disbelief. 'There are only nine plates.'

And suddenly there was pandemonium. From all sides people started shouting questions while cameramen and photographers pushed forward to get a better picture. The five attendants on either side quickly formed a cordon around Bosman and the painting.

'One at a time please', Bosman shouted, arms outspread. 'Ladies and gentleman please wait your turn.' Gradually the din died down. 'Thank you. Now, questions. You there, madam.'

'Do you know when the plate went missing?'

'Well, we are quite certain the plate was still there at closing time,' he said with a glance at Douwe. 'This morning we found it gone, so it must have happened during the night.'

Let him take the credit, Pieter thought. What I want to know is how in heaven's name this could have happened.

'So how do you explain this?' asked a reporter at the back, as if he had read Pieter's mind.

'Well, the police are of course still looking into the matter,' Bosman said, 'but I can tell you this much. So far we have not found any traces of a break-in, the alarm system didn't go off last night and there's no damage at all to the painting.'

'I'm sorry, sir,' the reporter at the back said, 'but what you just said makes it even more of a mystery.'

From then on the whole affair was referred to as *The Bruegel Mystery.*

7. The Jug

As soon as the news broke, people started gathering in front of the museum, eager to see the empty spot where the plate had been. But the museum remained closed for the rest of the day to allow the police to do their job.

Nevertheless, by four o'clock the museum square was filled with people and they started to lose their patience, which gave rise to some minor scuffles. From his office on the second floor the museum director, the head of police and the city councillor for culture watched as the police intervened.

'I can't remember the last time the museum drew such a crowd,' director Bosman said taking a nip from his whisky.

'It's a pity we're missing out on all those entrance fees,' the councillor said thinking of the urgent restoration works to the museum.

'If we do not open for the public tomorrow, there will be riots,' the head of police said puffing his cigar.

Their decision was unanimous: the next day the museum would re-open. But *The Peasant Wedding* was to be guarded like the crown juwels.

The following morning, as Pieter Douwe approached the museum, the queues reached as far as the petshop in Schilderstraat. The mood was tense. People had been forced off the museum square to make room for the world media which had turned out in full force.

All through the day the museum staff had barely time to breathe. One group of attendants had to bodysearch all visitors and confiscate umbrella's, spray cans, nail files, anything that looked remotely dangerous. Once inside other attendants took over charged with guiding the constant stream of visitors in small groups past the heavily guarded painting. People were hardly given the chance to look at the painting before they were rushed out to make room for the next group. On and on it went like that, the whole day long. By closing time the number of people still wanting to get in was such that the director, the councillor and the head of police decided to keep the museum open till 11 p.m.

It was almost midnight when Douwe came home. His knees hurt and it felt like a ton of bricks was weighing on his chest. Too tired to eat he switched the TV on and flopped down on the couch. The late news was on.

'... a spectacular new turn in the Bruegel Mystery,' the newscaster said.

In a flash Douwe was wide awake.

'The mysterious falsifier, if that's what we can call him, has struck again. This time in Vienna, in the Art History Museum, which boasts the largest collection of Bruegels in the world. Just like in Antwerp an object has simply disappeared from a painting. The work in question is Bruegel's *Peasant Dance*. This is what the painting looked like originally. Notice the jug on the table behind the bagpiper's back. Now look at the painting in its present state: the jug has gone. It was a musuem attendant who made the discovery.'

'Bettina!' Douwe exclaimed as a woman appeared on the screen. He knew Bettina quite well from his numerous visits to the Art History Museum. When on vacation Douwe always went to cities which had original Bruegels on show: Paris, Berlin, London, Madrid, New York... And so over the years he got well acquainted with a number of colleagues, each and every one of them Bruegel fanatics like him.

'The world media have flocked to Vienna,' the newscaster said, 'but so far they have precious little to report. Belgian and Austrian police have started a joint investigation into what they think is the work of an international crime syndicate.'

Hours later Douwe was still tossing and turning in bed. I have to try and catch some sleep, he thought, because tomorrow will be another tough day. But the same questions kept going through his head. Who was after his Bruegels and why? It was nearly dawn when he finally fell asleep..

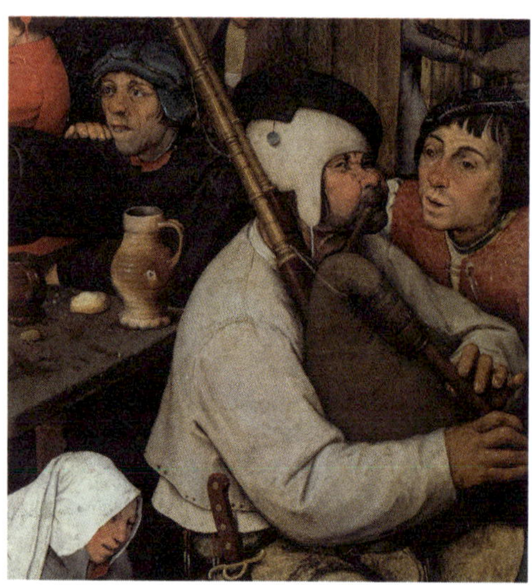

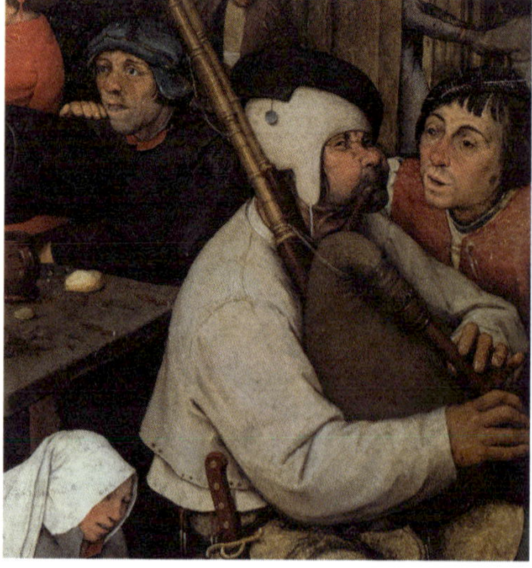

8. Caught

Douwe looked pale with fatigue and had pouches under his eyes but he didn't get time to rest because visitors kept coming. In the course of the afternoon his legs grew weak, he checked his watch for the hundredth time. Quarter to four, more than an hour to go, he wouldn't make it. He had to go and lie down before he fell down.

'Two minutes,' he whispered to a colleague while he pointed in the direction of the toilets. Turning the corner he made straight for the small storage room. The moment his head hit the couch, he was asleep.

Douwe woke up and looked at his watch. Half past four. He'd slept for just half an hour but the little nap had done him a world of good. He felt re-born, ready to confront the bustle outside. He straightened his uniform jacket, opened the door and was greeted by darkness and silence. For a moment he was at a loss. Where had everybody gone to? And then he got it. He had slept around the clock. It was half past four at night. The museum was deserted.

What now? He couldn't go home because as soon as he opened a door or a window, somewhere an alarm would go off. No, he knew what he was going to do. With all the fuss of the last couple of days he had hardly had time to look at his Bruegels. He went to the locker room and took out his torch. But he didn't switch it on just yet. He was able to find his way around the museum in pitch-darkness. Only as he stood in front of *The Peasant Wedding*, did he switch on the torch. It gave but little light. He hadn't thought of changing the batteries. The tenth plate was still missing. Slowly he moved the weak beam of light over to the wicker basket in the lower left corner. 'Unbelievable!' Douwe cried out. His voice echoed through the empty museum. He automatically switched off his torch. He thought he'd heard something. While he stood and listened he wondered if it could be true what he thought he'd seen. Burning with curiosity he switched on the torch but nothing happened. The batteries were dead. 'O no, not now!' he moaned. 'Light,' he called, 'give me light!'

He jumped as the overhead lights switched on.

'Don't move!' someone called out.

Douwe closed his eyes against the bright light and heard heavy boots coming his way. By the time four policemen grabbed him, his eyes had adjusted to the light. He was right! There, in the wicker basket, lay an additional jug. The jug from Vienna, he knew with absolute certainty. He was so excited he hardly felt he was being handcuffed. He could already see the headlines: *Vienna jug turns up in Antwerp* or *Objects travelling between paintings.*

'Director!' Douwe cried as he noticed Bosman talking to two men in plain clothes. 'Just the person I need.'

'Why am I not surprised it's you again, Douwe,' Bosman sighed. Judging by his dishevelled hair the director had been called out of bed. He was in a foul mood. 'These are detective inspector Beckx and detective sergeant Janssen,' he said to Douwe. 'Just answer their questions so that I can go back to bed.'

'Do you know the suspect, director? Beckx asked.

'I'm afraid I do. This is Pieter Douwe, museum attendant.'

'Janssen,' Beckx ordered, 'have the premises searched.'

'I found it,' Douwe said excitedly to the director.

'Here we go again,' Bosman said.

'It's in the wicker basket.'

'What are you talking about, Douwe?

'The jug. I'm talking about the jug. It's here!'

'What jug?' said Bosman, who couldn't make head or tail of it.

'Do I get to ask questions too by any chance?' detective Beckx cut in.

'My apologies, inspector,' Bosman said. 'Please go ahead.'

'The jug from Vienna,' Douwe said.

'Douwe, shut up and answer the questions!' Bosman shouted.

'No-one else in the building, sir,' detective Janssen said as he returned to the hall.

'Any signs of breaking and entering?'

'Negative, sir.'

'So how did you get in, mister Douwe?' Beckx asked.

'I didn't get in. I mean, I was still in.'

'I see,' Beckx said. 'You let yourself be locked in.'

'Locked in?' Bosman said.

'Perpetrator hides inside till the doors are closed,' Janssen quoted from the text book.

'You sly old fox,' Bosman said.

'Fortunately this time the motion sensors did their job,' Beckx said. 'I still don't get why the alarm didn't go off the night the plate of pie disappeared. Anyway, this time we caught our man redhanded. Janssen, take him along for questioning.'

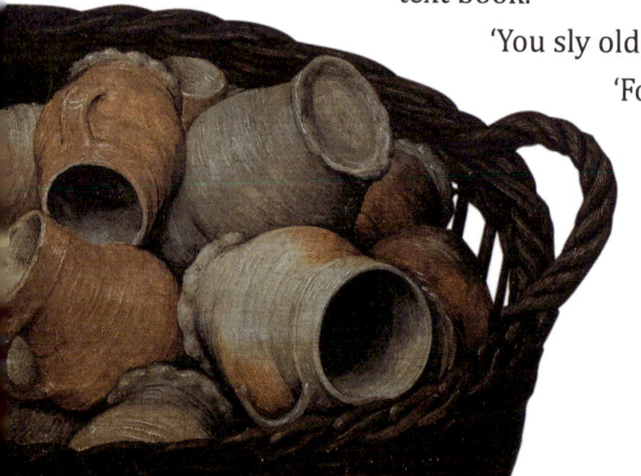

9. Circus tent

'But boys,' Miss Vriends exclaimed, 'it's happening in your own city and you do not know a thing about it?' She showed us a photograph of *The Peasant Wedding*. 'Here were ten plates of pie. Now there are only nine. The one that stood here has disappeared.'

My jaw dropped. That was the plate I had taken off the tray. It had to be there somewhere because I dropped it when Freddy brought me back.

'And in Vienna too an object went missing from a Bruegel painting,' Vriends went on.' I knew before she even showed us *The Peasant Dance*, that it was the jug I had taken behind the bagpiper's back.

'The police are doing everything they can to catch whoever is behind this.'

I looked around nervously, sure that I was betraying myself as the culprit, but all eyes were on miss Vriends. The only one looking at me was Freddy, who gave me a stealthy thumbs-up.

'So far nobody has a clue what happened,' Vriends said. 'The police are looking into the matter. So before long we may learn what really happened. But we are

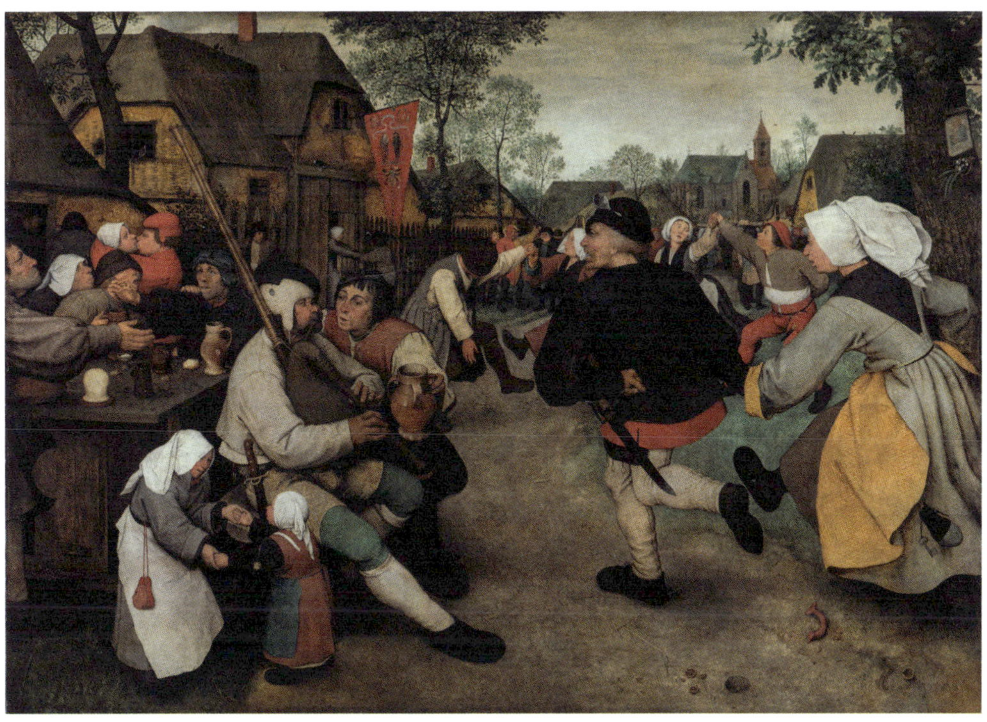

not going to wait for that.' She pauzed and the whole class held its breath. 'We are going to find out for ourselves. That is your new assignment. Write a composition in which you give an explanation for the Bruegel mystery. How do you think this happened? Who do you think is behind this? You're to hand in your compositions on Monday. And remember, boys, give your imagination free rein!'

I sat by the swimming pool, knees pulled up and shivering. Floating in the water beside me was Freddy. His belly ballooned in his blue and white swimming trunks. The rest of the class were at the deep end of the pool, pushing each other off the springboard, holding each other under water and generally behaving like the savages they were.

'The Bruegel Mystery,' I mumbled teeth chattering. 'It's all my doing.'

'Yes, isn't it fantastic!' Freddy said gleefully. 'You made world news! But apart from you and I nobody knows who's behind it.'

'Teugels, get in the water,' Boxer shouted.

I didn't like swimming. Actually, I managed pretty well as long as I knew I was able to touch bottom, but any deeper than that and panic set in. Ever so carefully I lowered myself into the pool, holding my breath as the cold water crept up my body.

'So what are you going to write in your composition, Benny boy?' Freddy asked.

'Good question. I can't tell the truth, that's for sure.'

'Why can't you?'

'Are you nuts? And give myself away?'

'A boy walking around in a painting, who's going to believe that?'

Freddy had a point. Just as I was about to tell him so, his eyes grew wide and he went under water. Somebody was pulling him by his legs, but in the swirling water I couldn't make out who it was. A few moments later the mystery boy swam away, while Freddy surfaced, gasping and coughing. At the far side of the pool the other boys stood watching. Cheers went up as a hand slowly rose out of the water. It held something limp and white and blue. Like a dolphin Jeff burst up to his middle out of the water.

'Circus tent!' he yelled.

And then it dawned on me what Jeff was holding up like a trophy. Freddy's swimming trunks!

'Circus tent! Circus tent! Circus tent!' the boys shouted in unison. Someone started the Batman tune and the swimming pool hall reverberated with Freddy's nickname. 'Fatman! Fatman!'

The only one who didn't join in was Sebastian. But I was sure this sick prank was his idea. This was his revenge for the penalty that Freddy had made him miss.

The chanting stopped abruptly when Boxer entered the hall.

'Allright, boys, go and get dressed,' he shouted.

But I couldn't leave Freddy in the lurch. He was still standing in the water, his back towards the rest of us, his hands clasped in front of him. He didn't make a sound but I saw his shoulders were shaking.

'Stadman and Teugels,' Boxer yelled, 'didn't you hear me? Get dressed, I said!'

I climbed out of the pool and looked around for Freddy's trunks. Behind the glass partition leading to the dressing cubicles, the boys stood and watched in amusement. For a moment I was afraid Jeff had taken his trophee with him, but then I saw the trunks hanging from the tip of the springboard. What a relief! It meant I need not venture into the deep to fetch them. The moment I set foot on the springboard, it started to bounce. I almost lost my balance and to my horror the trunks fell in the water.

'Teugels, what are you trying to achieve?' said Dhondt calmly, not the loud-mouthed Boxer for once. I startled and fell off the board. As the water engulfed me panic tightened my throat. I thrashed around looking for a hold, but which way was up and which way was down? I opened my eyes wide and suddenly Dhondt's face floated into view. I saw bubbles coming out of his mouth as he said something I could not understand. He turned me around, grabbed me under my armpits and with two powerful kicks of his legs brought my head above water. I gasped for air.

'Get hold of the ridge, Ben.' It was the first time Dhondt called me by my first name. 'We are going to get these swimming trunks, you hear? We will show those boys that you can do this.'

It felt like a victory when, a few minutes later, I climbed the ladder holding Freddy's trunks.

'You see, Ben, you can do more than you think,' said Dhondt. As he turned around, he became Boxer again. 'Okay, you monkeys,' he cried, 'the circus is over. But not for Jeff the clown, he will have some explaining to do to the headmaster.'

10. Lazy-Luscious-Land

'I could eat a horse', Freddy said as we sat down for dinner. He had hardly spoken a word since the swimming pool incident earlier that day. But the sight of his favourite meal, meatballs, apple sauce and mashed potatoes, cheered him up considerably.

'I say, Fat Freddy,' Jeff called out after supervisor De Letter had left, 'does your circus tent still fit after that little mishap?'

The refectory fell silent and all heads turned our way. Freddy, who was about to furtively put a meatball in his mouth, froze. I didn't know what came over me but everything turned red before my eyes. I'd had enough of Freddy being bullied and humiliated. I felt pent-up rage rise up in me like lava in a volcano. My body started to move of its own free will. You could hear a pin drop as I walked, fists clenched, over to where Jeff sat next to Sebastian. I knew it was him, Sebastian, who was calling the shots. Jeff was merely the puppet that carried out whatever the puppet-master wanted him to.

'Help!' Jeff yelped. 'Somebody help me. Save me from the mad midget.'

I stopped right in front of them. Sebastian gave me a look of amused surprise. Jeff sat there smiling but I saw his muscles twitch, ready to parry me the moment I struck out. So instead of going for Jeff I grabbed Sebastian's head and pushed it face down into a bowl of apple sauce. His head veered up straight away, his face dripping with apple sauce. The boys roared with laughter.

'You'll pay for this,' Sebastian hissed. But just as he was about to take a swing at me, a meatball hit him square between the eyes. We all looked to where the missile had come from. There was Freddy, leaning backwards to put his full weight into his next throw. He let go of the meatball and it hit Jeff smack on the nose. 'Bull's eye!' Freddy cheered.

Seconds later all hell broke loose. Meatballs were flying in all directions as the boys screamed and hooted with laughter. Some climbed on the tables to lay their hands on more ammunition. Bowls of apple sauce fell to the ground. Others started throwing handfulls of potato mash. The noise was deafening.

In the middle of it all Freddy stood plucking meatballs from the air with hands the size of baseball gloves. He stuffed them in his pockets and every now and then one in his mouth.

'Stop!' De Letter screamed at the top of his voice as he came charging into the refectory. 'Stop it now!' The racket died down, the silence only broken by one more thud as another meatball hit the floor, which caused some snickering.

'Silence!' De Letter shouted. He had to watch his step because the floor was littered with squashed meatballs and smears of mash and apple sauce. 'Just look at this pigsty! Right, who started this?'

The boys all looked at their feet.

'It's your choice, you can either tell me or all go to bed without food.'

To my surprise nobody snitched on me, not even Sebastian. But I did not want them to think I was too much of a coward to own up.

'I started it, sir,' I said.

'It wasn't Ben, sir,' Freddy said before De Letter got the chance of giving me a piece of his mind. 'I started it.'

'So you both want to take the blame? Suit yourselves. No dinner for you two.'

I looked at Freddy, thinking this had to come as a blow to him. Missing out on his favourite meal. But to my surprise he smiled mysteriously.

'Well, what are you waiting for? Off to bed.'

As Freddy put one foot forward, a meatball fell out of his trouser leg. There was stifled laughter.

'Just a minute, Stadman', De Letter said.

Freddy froze and the smile disappeared from his face.

'Empty your pockets!'

Reluctantly Freddy dug up a meatball and put it on the table.

'All of them,' said De Letter.

As the meatballs kept coming from a variety of pockets, the pile on the table grew as did the laughter. De Letter watched as Freddy gave up all of his spoils, then he restored order.

'Silence!' he bellowed. 'Stadman and Teugels, off to bed. As for the rest of you, there's your dinner spread out, you can eat off the floor, like the pigs you are.'

'I don't think I will last till morning.' Freddy lay on his bed clutching his stomach. 'I'm dying of hunger.'

'I think there's little chance of that happening,' I said. 'But to be rid of your wailing, I'll go and get you something to eat.'

'Are you crazy? If De Letter catches you in the kitchen...'

'The kitchen? Who's talking about the kitchen?' I took the Bruegel book from under my mattress and showed Freddy the picture of *Lazy-Luscious-Land*. 'Just look at these men sleeping. They certainly had their fill.'

'I'm sure I won't. You can go and eat as much as you like, while I stay here, starving.'

'No, no. I'll bring you something. That's a promise. I've been reading what it says in the book about the painting. Shall I tell you what's on the menu?'

'I'm all ears.'

'To get into *Lazy-Luscious-Land* you have to eat your way through a mountain of pie, just like that little fellow in the upper right-hand corner.'

'Piece of cake,' Freddy said.

'And then there's abundance. You can have some pork. No need to look for a knife, the good animal obligingly carries one in its side. Or do you prefer goose? Look, it's laying itself on a plate, roasted and all. You can have sausages as well. The fences, you see, are made of them. Do you want some bread to go with it, these cactuses are actually round loaves. And there's no shortage of pies, as you can see on the roof. So, what do you want?'

Freddy had to swallow before he was able to speak. 'All of it. I want all of it.'

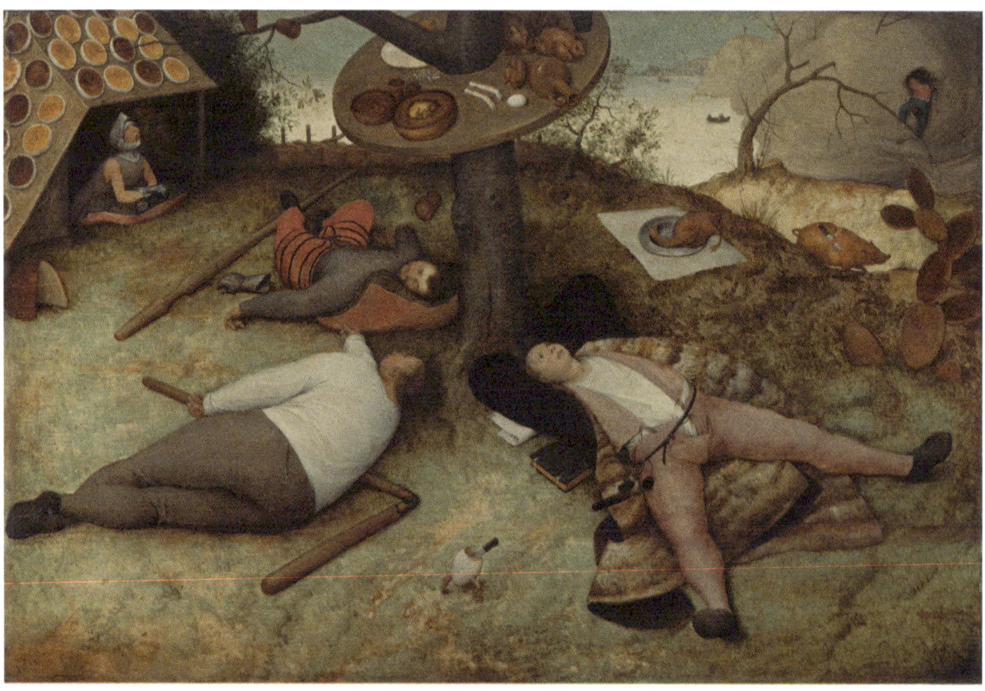

11. Well-earned rest

Pieter Douwe was a free man again. The police had kept him locked up for twenty-four hours, during which time detectives Beckx and Janssen had grilled him repeatedly. It was hard on an old man like Douwe and during the last interview he had become unwell.

And now, all of a sudden he was out in the street. The police had not given an explanation for his release. But everything became clear when he passed a kiosk.

Lazy-Luscious-Land Plundered said one newspaper.

Munich: Bruegel Mystery Widens another one said.

Douwe bought a copy of every paper and hurried home.

Five sausages, two loaves of bread and three pies. That was what had gone missing from *Lazy-Luscious-Land*. There was no mention of Douwe's name. But then he had a cast-iron alibi: he had been in police custody when the painting was plundered. No mention either of the jug Douwe had seen the night of his arrest. He had tried to tell it to Bosman but it looked like the director had not understood him. Or had he, Douwe, just imagined it? He had to go and check.

Douwe had forgotten it was the museum's closing day but that turned out to be a blessing. A cleaning lady had let him in. After the hectic past few days the silence in the museum was heavenly.

One look at *The Peasant Wedding* told him he had not been mistaken. In the wicker basket in the lower lefthand corner was a jug that hadn't been there before, it was the jug that had gone missing in Vienna, he'd stake his life on it.

So what Douwe now knew and nobody else seemed to know was that it wasn't just a matter of objects disappearing. Here was something that had been added to a painting.

And then a thought struck him. What if there was more? What if other things had appeared without anyone noticing? He would find out straight away. So once again Douwe let his eyes wander over the painting of *The Peasant Wedding*. The long line of guests eating and drinking at the table, the bagpipers, it was all so familiar to him. The bustle at the barn gate... Wait a minute, something wasn't right there. But he couldn't quite put his finger on it. There were so many people packed together, all one could see were heads. And then he saw it, an extra head in the crowd, a head that had not been there before. It was just a dot of scarlet paint without any

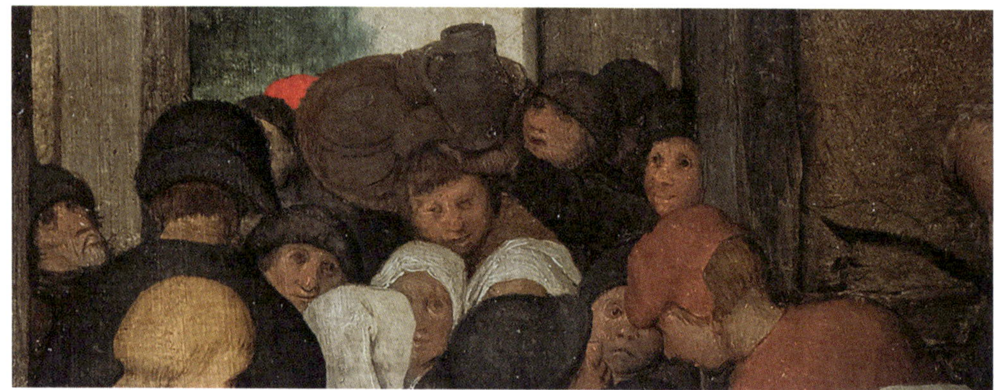

features. So it had to be the back of a head, the head of someone leaving the barn. A man's head to be precise, because only men wore coloured caps. The women all wore white headscarves. So there, leaving the barn, was a man with a red cap who had not been in the painting before.

'I thought I'd find you here,' said a voice behind him. Douwe started and swung round, director Bosman was coming towards him. 'Still sticking your nose in the Bruegels, are you?' he said with a forced smile. 'Nevertheless, I'm happy they set you free, Pieter.'

It was the first time ever that Bosman adressed him by his first name. Douwe didn't like the sound of that.

'The thing is, Pieter, I didn't know how long they were going to keep you. Indeed, I didn't even know if you were coming back at all. And given the fact that you've already got forty years of service…'

'Forty-one!'

'Right, forty or forty-one. What's the difference? Long enough at any rate to deserve some well-earned rest.'

'I don't want any rest,' Douwe exclaimed. 'I want to be with my Bruegels.'

'Your Bruegels?' Bosman shouted. 'These paintings do not belong to you! In fact, you needn't worry about them anymore. I've appointed a new museum attendant, because you are retired as of today!'

Douwe felt a stab in his heart and for a second everything went black. To take his Bruegels away from him after decades of dedication! Tears pricked behind his eyes.

'Of course you're still free to come and see the Bruegels,' Bosman said in a softer tone of voice, 'but only during opening hours, like any ordinary visitor.'

Without a word Douwe turned his back on the director. As he opened the exit doors, his mind was set. He would start his own investigation…Tomorrow…In Vienna.

.12. The Accident

The day of the accident started off well enough. That morning in class miss Vriends handed out our graded compositions.

'Freddy, you did not hand in any assignment. Is that correct?'

'Yes, miss. I've been ill.'

'Too many meatballs, no doubt,' Jeff said loud enough to set the boys off laughing.

It wasn't meatballs, I thought, but lots of sausages and even more pies.

The one boy who didn't laugh, was Sebastian. When it came to marks he was deadly serious. He had a reputation to keep up of being the best at everything, so time and again he handed in the best compositions.

Miss Vriends didn't call out our names in alphabetical order but worked her way up from the boy with the lowest marks. Most of the time that was Jeff.

'Jeff, you obviously made no effort at all. Your explanation for the Bruegel Mystery is feeble, to say the least, and your language is untidy as always: clumsy sentences and lots of spelling mistakes.'

I usually didn't do too well either. Not that I got unsatisfactory marks, it was just that most courses did not interest me enough for me to make an effort. But this time was different, this time I was on tenterhooks. I'd spent practically the whole weekend writing and re-writing my composition and had even enjoyed it. It wasn't easy to make a good story out of all the images and ideas that tumbled through my head. But once it was finished, I had this wonderful feeling of satisfaction. So it meant a lot to me what Miss Vriends would have to say about my composition.

She was already down to the boys with the best marks and my name still hadn't come up. Eventually there were only two left.

'So it's between Sebastian and Ben,' Vriends said.

I held my breath as she took her time to continue.

'Sebastian,' she said.

His face lit up and he balled a fist in triumph.

'Splendid work as always. Good style, fluent sentences, impeccable spelling...'

All right, all right, I thought. That's enough praise for today. We don't want him to burst with pride, do we?

'But your story is rather boring.'

Did she just say *boring*? She must have, by the look on Sebastian's face.

'You give a reasonable explanation for the mystery, Sebastian, but it lacks inspiration, imagination. That's what makes good stories, imagination, and there's plenty of that in Ben's composition. So that's why this time the top marks go to Ben Teugels!'

I turned red as the whole class looked at me. Freddy gave me the broadest of smiles. As to Sebastian, if looks could kill I would have died then and there.

'The explanation Ben comes up with,' Vriends explained, 'is the most imaginative one I've read. A boy ends up in Bruegel's painting and takes away a plate of pie. It's both fantastic and yet so simple, so… plausible.'

I felt my cheeks glow with pride.

'What's more, your story reads fluently, the way you bring Bruegel's painting to life with mere words, is quite admirable. It almost feels as if you've been there

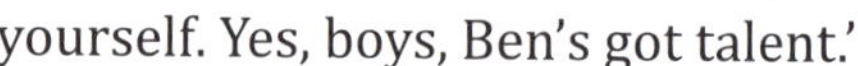

yourself. Yes, boys, Ben's got talent.'

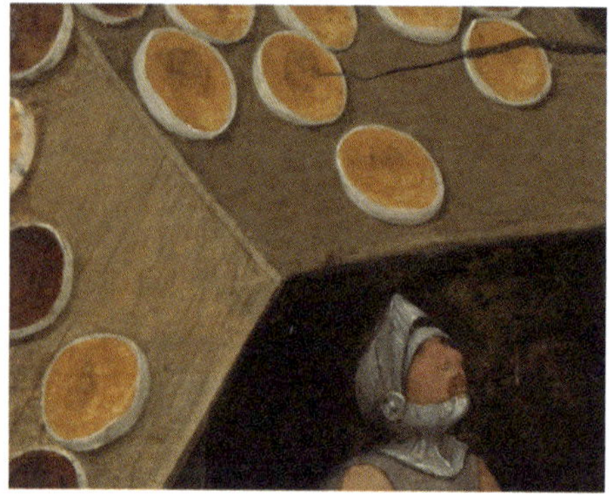

Later that day we went into the city for an orientation exercise. Armed with a compass and a map Freddie and I were walking along Nationale Straat.

'Ladies and gentlemen,' Freddy said out loud, 'here goes a talented boy.' Some passers-by looked our way.

'Stop it, Freddy. Or I shall be forced to write another composition in which I describe how you stuffed yourself with all the food I brought from *Lazy-Luscious-Land.*

'O please,' said Freddy, 'do not remind me of these delicacies. Not while I'm starving. I need something to sink my teeth into. Isn't there a pastry shop hereabouts?' He looked up and down the street and stopped dead in his tracks. 'O God! Look who's there.'

Sebastian and Jeff were coming our way.

'We'd better steer clear of these two for a while,' I said.

'Quickly, let's cross the street before they spot us.' And with that Freddy just stepped into the road from behind a parked van. The flash of a passing car, tyres shrieking, a dull thud and Freddy was gone.

From then on everything seemed to happen in slow motion. People came running and shouting. They stopped the traffic and bent over a pile of clothes lying in the road. The clothes looked familiar. An ambulance arrived. People in orange suits jumped out and kneeled down by the pile of clothes. One of them got a stretcher from the ambulance. As they lifted the pile of clothes onto the stretcher, I realized it was Freddy who was being pushed into the ambulance.

'Freddy?' I croaked. I wanted to go over but somebody stopped me. The ambulance tore away. The wailing siren seemed to wake me up.

'Ben! Ben, can you hear me?' Sebastian was shaking me. 'It's no use staying here, Ben. You'd better come with me. I'll bring you back to school.'

13. The Intruder

At five p.m. sharp Pieter Douwe pushed the bell at the service entrance of the Art History Museum in Vienna. Thirty seconds later the door opened and Bettina stuck her head out.

'Hello, Pieter, do come in,' she said as she looked left and right down the street and quickly closed the door behind him.

'You look tired, Pieter. Those days in prison must have been hard on you.'

'I'll live.'

'So what exactly are you looking for? You didn't want to tell me over the phone.'

'Well, Bettina, if you don't mind, I'll keep it to myself until I've found more evidence. Because my theory is so far out I have difficulty believing it myself.'

'You do make me curious, Pieter. But we had better go straight to the Bruegel hall then, because there isn't much time, one hour is all I can give you.'

In the Bruegel hall the last visitors were being ushered out.

'I leave you to it, Pieter,' said Bettina. 'Remember, just one hour and then I have to throw you out as well.'

Douwe looked around the hall. Here was the biggest collection of Bruegels in the world. He had one hour to find out if something new had appeared in any of them, like it had in *The Peasant Wedding.*

'Any success?' Bettina asked as she returned fifty-five minutes later.

'Come and see.' Pieter walked over to *The Peasant Dance*. 'Look here.' He pointed out a dot of scarlet paint behind the dancing couple in the background, the one raising their arms.

'I don't believe it,' Bettina exclaimed. 'That wasn't there before.'

'What do you make of it?'

'I don't know. Let's see... A head? It must be a man's head cause he's wearing a cap. I'd say it's a man with a red cap walking away from the dancing peasants.'

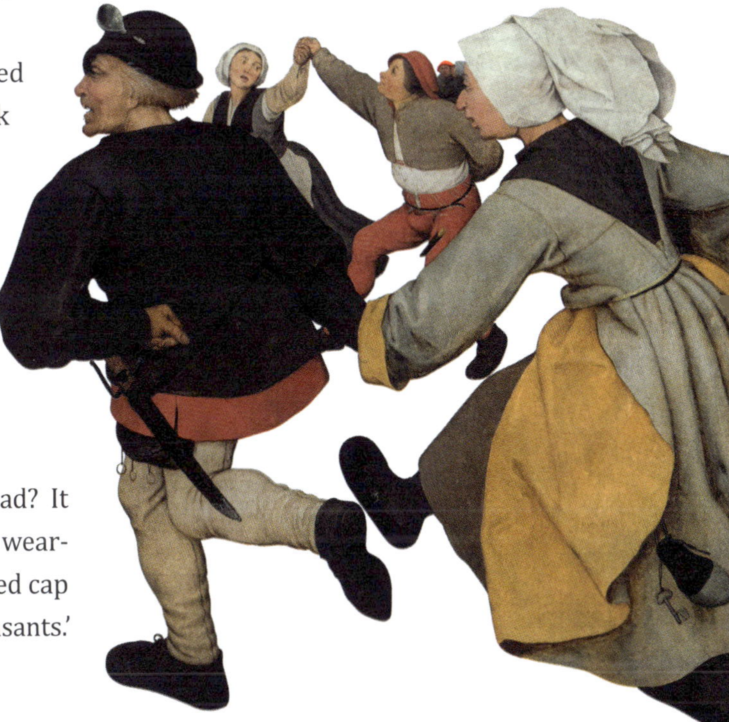

'My thoughts exactly. And you know what, Bettina? Yesterday I spotted the same scarlet dot in *The Peasant Wedding*.'

'You can't be serious! Do you mean to say someone is adding dots of paint to our Bruegels? Who would do such a thing?'

'I think Bruegel does it.'

'Bruegel?' Bettina exclaimed.

'Yes. I've thought long and hard about his, Bettina, and I think Bruegel is calling for our help.'

'Pieter, you're talking in riddles. Are you saying Bruegel wants you and me to help him?'

'You and me and all our colleagues who have Bruegels in their care. After all, are we not the guardians of his masterpieces?'

'You bet we are. But what does he need our help for?'

'He wants us to find the intruder.'

'The intruder?'

'Yes. Obviously someone here and now has found a way to get into his paintings. And that someone is ruining his works. First it was only a plate but now it's downright plundering. Where is it going to stop? Unless we put a stop to it. Bruegel wants that intruder out of the picture. He wants us to track him down.'

'That's all very well, Pieter. But tell me, how are we to achieve what the combined police forces of Belgium, Austria and Germany are unable to do?'

'The difference is, my dear Bettina, that we get a little help from our friend. Bruegel is giving us hints, small hints that anybody else will overlook. He doesn't want the whole world to see. There's enough commotion as it is.'

'But how can he give us hints if he cannot talk to us?'

'He can talk to us. He is talking to us through his pictures. He's giving us glimpses of the intuder.'

'Now I see what you're getting at,' Bettina said. 'You think the man with the red cap is the intruder.'

'Exactly. The intruder stole a plate of pie at *The Peasant Wedding* and Bruegel shows him leaving the barn.'

'He grabbed a jug at *The Peasant Dance*,' Bettina continued, 'and Bruegel shows him walking away from the dancing peasants. So tell me, did you find any trace of our man in any of the other paintings?'

'I'm afraid not. Unless... I have one more to go. *Hunters in the Snow*.'

'You'd better be quick about it then,' said Bettina checking her watch, 'because

I have to activate the alarm system.'

Four eyes went over the painting. But there was no sign of the red-capped intruder. Bettina tapped her watch.

'We really have to go now.'

'Okay,' Douwe sighed. But just as he was about to turn his back on the painting, he noticed one of the dogs was no longer sniffing the snow, it was looking at something. Douwe followed its stare and there he was, hardly discernible amid the shrubbery. The dog had seen him too: the red-capped intruder.

That same night, from her appartment, Bettina and Douwe called all their colleagues, Bruegel fanatics each and every one of them. Without giving too much away – because the telephone had ears – they asked them to carefully examine their Bruegels.

New York was first to react with news about *The Harvesters*. It was easily missed between all that golden corn, but to the left of the first harvester a man with a red cap came peeping out of the corn field.

Berlin, London, Paris and Madrid didn't have anything unusual to report. But Munich had discovered an interesting detail about the already ravaged *Lazy-Luscious-Land*. The little fellow that ate himself a way through a mountain of pie, used to wear a brown cap. Now it was red!

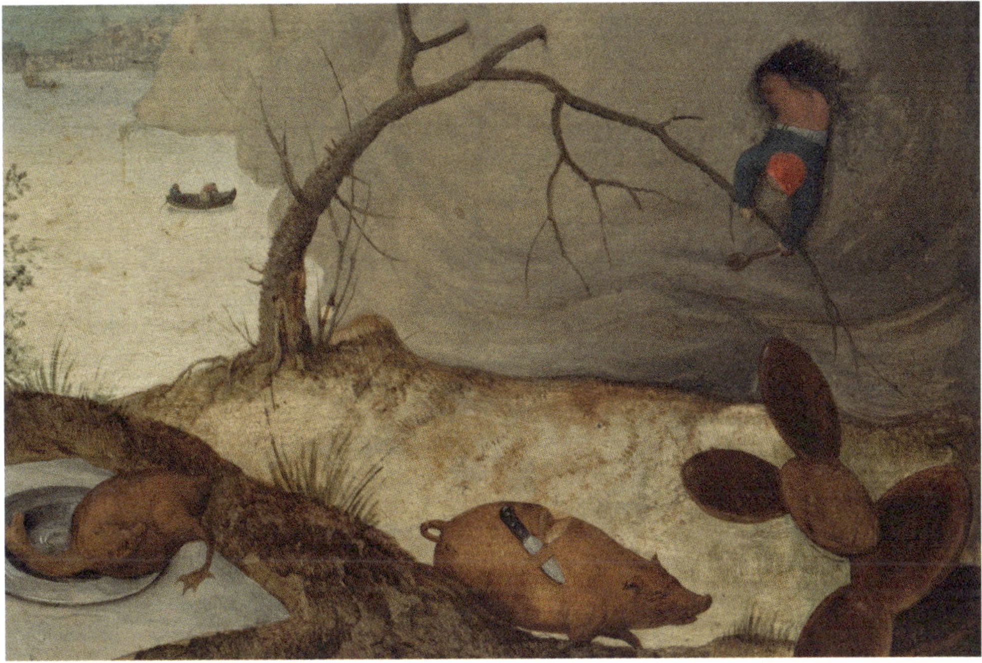

14. The Cripples

I woke with a sob.

'It's all right, Ben.' Miss Vriends was sitting by my bed. Why was I in bed during the day? Why did I feel so terribly sad? And then I remembered.

'Freddy,' I moaned. 'Where's Freddy? I want to see him.'

'You can't go and see him just yet, Ben. He's unconscious but the doctors said he'll be all right. You try and get some sleep now and tomorrow, I promise you, we will go to the hospital to see your friend.'

It was the first time somebody called Freddy my friend. I don't know if that's what brought it on but all of a sudden I burst into tears. Miss Vriends took me into her arms. Her motherly embrace, her sweet smell, her soothing voice reminded me so much of mama I started wailing uncontrollably. It was as if years of pent-up grief came rushing out. In between howls and helpless blubbering I tried to tell her how much I missed my parents and my dog, Max. How I had felt so lonely for so long till I found a friend in Freddy. But then he too met with an accident, I was cursed. Everything, everyone I grew attached to, was snatched away from me.

I'm not sure Miss Vriends was able to make head or tail of it, because it all came out in bits and pieces. Her clothes must have been covered in snot and tears, but she kept rocking me gently and stroking my hair, until I had spat it all out. I felt spent and empty and strangely relieved. And I wished she would hold me like this forever.

I must have dozed off, for when I opened my eyes, Miss Vriends was gone. On seeing Freddy's empy bed, sadness crept back up on me. I knew only one cure: Rex.

This time the dog was not at his master's feet, perhaps he was somewhere outside. In front of the barn the peasants danced to a jolly tune but I was not in the mood for that. So I quickly turned a corner and found myself in a dark alley. The gloom of the place suited me and so I trudged along, head bent to the ground, deeper and deeper into a labyrinth of alleyways.

Turning yet another corner I ran into a group of cripples blocking the way. if only I had Rex with me. The bearded one with the red helmet pointed at my neck and said something I couldn't understand. He seemed to be the leader for on his signal they all started to hobble towards me on their primitive crutches. Their voices were hoarse, their teeth rotten, their eyes glistening with greed. Before I knew it they had me cornered. The stench of their clothes made me gag. With a quick movement the cripple with the red helmet hooked his crutch behind my dummy stone and pulled hard. Bending my head I let the shoelace slide over it.

As the cripples started clubbing each other to get hold of the pebble stone, I made a run for it, down the maze of alleyways. After a while it dawned on me there was no way the cripples could keep up with me. I stood there, panting, as darkness fell and I had absolutely no idea which way to go. No dog to show me the way, no dummy stone to bring me back and Freddy unconscious in hospital. My legs gave way and I started to cry. I was stuck in the sixteenth century.

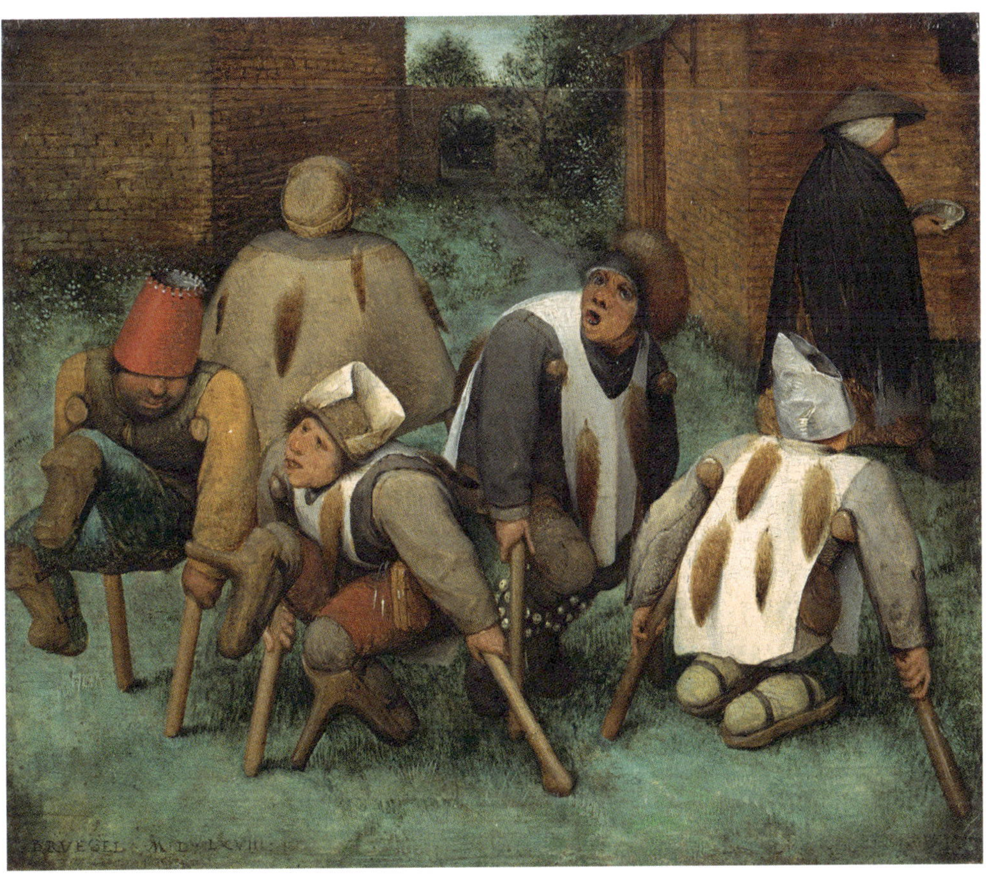

15. Déjà-vu

Douwe hadn't slept a wink on Bettina's hard sofa. He had planned to catch up on his sleep on the return flight from Vienna, but something kept nagging him. He felt he had overlooked something.

He was hot on the heels of the intruder now. That same morning Paris had called to say that the man with the red cap had now shown up in *The Cripples* as well. One could just see the back of him as he fled into an alleyway. The net is closing, Douwe thought, thanks to his colleagues all over the world. All over the world? But what about Antwerp? There were still some paintings in the museum that had not been examined!

On landing he did not listen to the little voice inside him that said he had better go home and rest. From the airport he took a taxi straight to the museum.

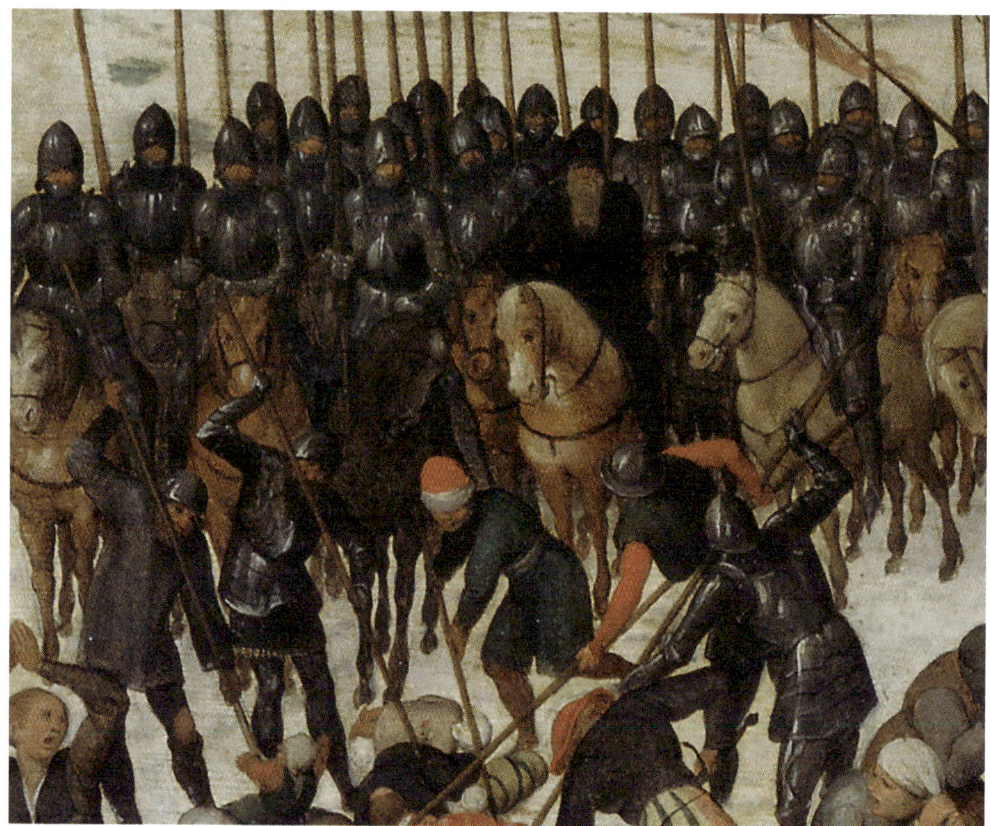

It felt funny to see another attendant in the Bruegel hall. His successor, a young woman, did not lose sight of Douwe as he studied *The Massacre of the Innocents.* He looked for the intruder among the people in the square. He checked if there wasn't a red-capped head that came peeping from behind a tree, the corner of a house or through a door or a window. All in vain. And even though a red cap would stick out like a sore thumb among the horsemen in grey armour, Douwe took a closer look at them just to make sure. All the soldiers sat and watched the slaughter, all except one. That soldier looked straight ahead, as if he was looking at someone outside the painting. Someone who had stood where Douwe now stood.

'Keep your distance, please sir,' the young woman called out.

And suddenly Douwe had a déjà-vu, the distinct feeling he had experienced the exact same situation before. Only, he had been the one shouting a warning from where the woman was standing. And right here, where he stood, was this pupil of Miss Vriends'. The one who had been laughed at. For being a redhead!

In a flash the jig-saw pieces fit into place. The intruder wasn't a man wearing a red cap but a boy with red hair. And Douwe knew exactly where to find him. Tired though he was, he danced for joy.

'I'm sorry, sir,' the attendant said, 'this is a museum, not a ballroom.'

'You are ever so right,' Douwe said. 'And I am very pleased to see that my Bruegels are in good hands.'

The woman watched in bewilderment as Douwe staggered out of the hall.

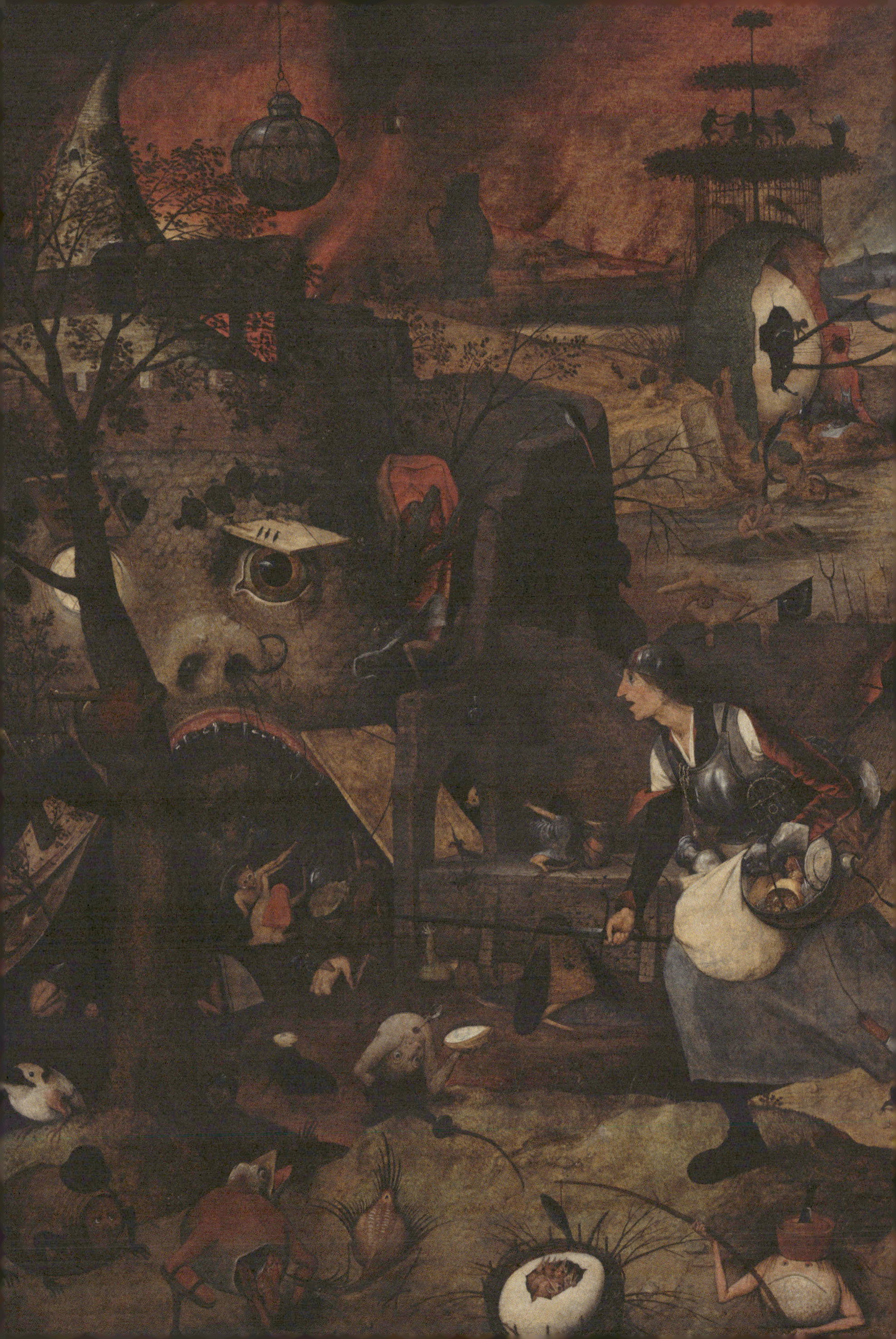

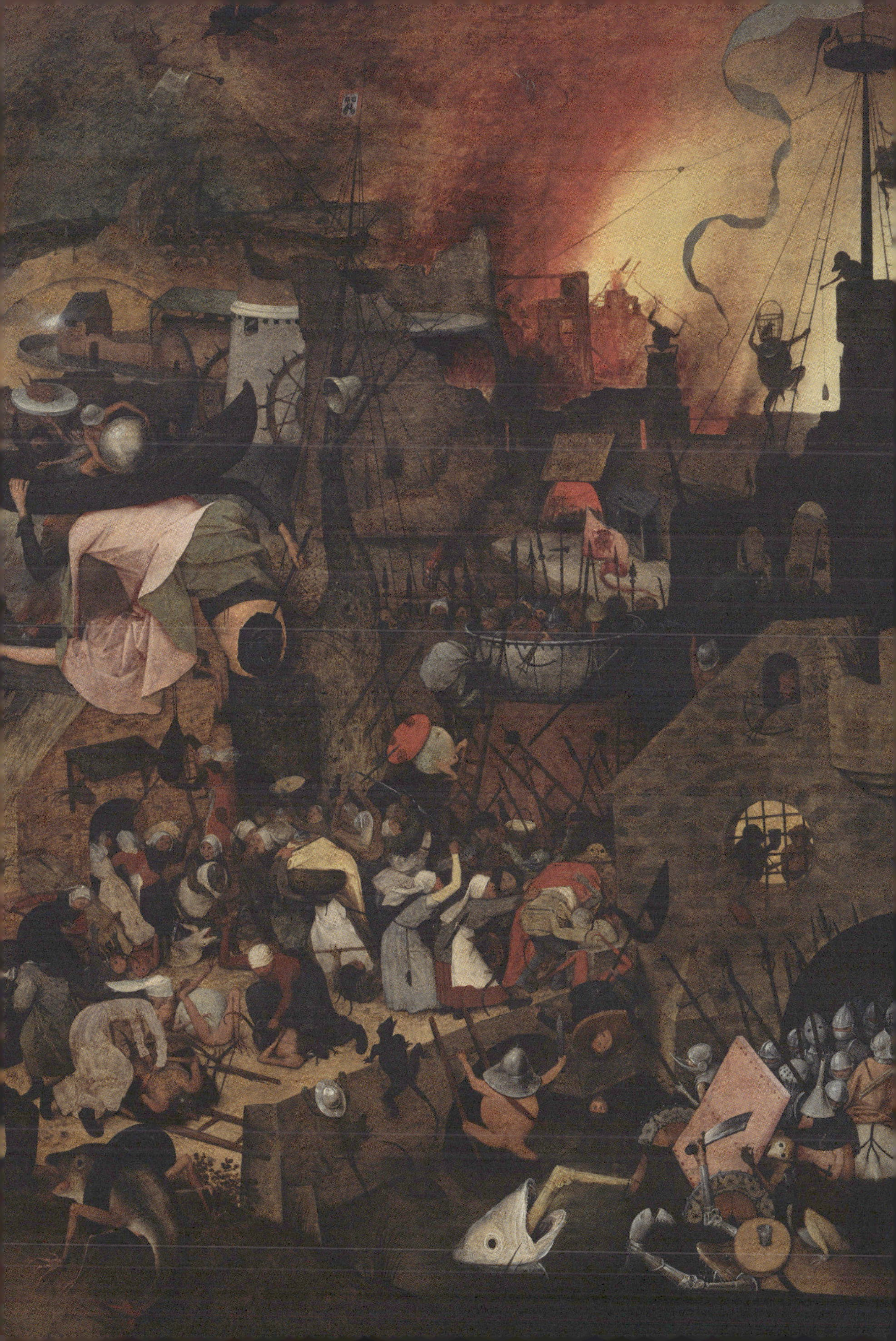

16. Mad Meg

It was no use whining, I had to find my own way back to the wedding barn. At least I would be warm there and have something to eat and drink.

It was pitch dark by now, with one hand to the wall I started to feel my way forward. I turned a corner and another, then another. And just as I thought I was walking in circles, I saw a faint beam of light cut into the darkness. I walked towards it and to my great joy found myself in an open space. I had found my way out of the maze of alleyways. In the distance a red glow spilled over a hilltop like sunrise over the horizon. It gave just enough light for me to see a path leading up there. Sloping gently initially, it then became steeper and steeper. But I didn't let it slow me down because by now I heard voices. They must have come from the peasant wedding. By the sound of it things there had gotten seriously out of hand, people were shrieking and bawling. Panting like an exhausted dog I reached the top and I beheld… hell!

At a glance I recognized Bruegel's *Mad Meg*. When leafing through the book I always quickly turned the page for fear of ending up in it. Now Bruegel's dreadful phantasy came to life before my very eyes.

I wanted to run. But I was paralyzed with fear.

I wanted to shut my eyes tight. But they were almost popping from their sockets as I watched the giant woman in armour, brandishing her sword and carrying a rattling collection of pots and pans.

I covered my ears. But still I heard the horrifying screams coming out of thousands of throats.

I felt the blistering heat of hellfire on my skin.

I smelt the nauseating stench of sulphur and scorched flesh.

Something touched my leg. I looked down. A creature with an upturned head for a body offered me a bowl of pie, a spoon in its mouth. Or was that its arse?

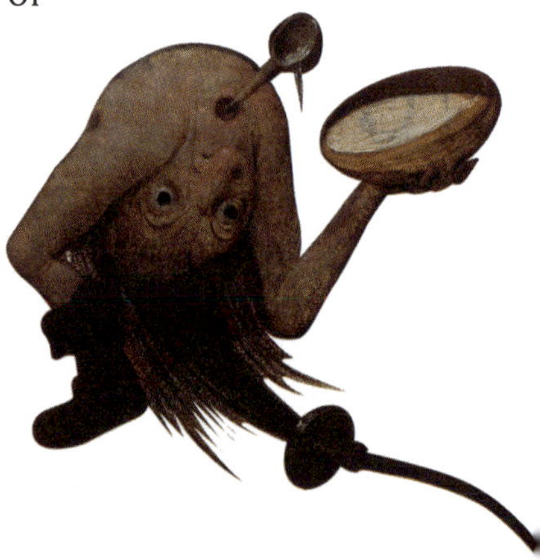

I screamed a glass shattering scream. The creature started screaming along and the spoon fell on my feet. They suddenly started running, pulling my body along. Faster and faster I went down the slope until I lost my balance, falling and tumbling into a ditch. There I lay, shivering with cold and fear and against my better judgement, I began to beg Freddy to get me out of there.

'O Freddy, please bring me back. Please, Freddy, please...'

17. Gibberish

Douwe got a sharp poke in the ribs.

'Wake up, sir. We're there.'

'Err, what's the matter?' For a moment Douwe did not know where he was.

'This is the address you gave me,' the taxi driver said impatiently. 'Prince Albert's? The boarding school?'

Oh yes, now he remembered. He was here to see the boy with the red hair. It had only been a short ride from the museum to the school and yet in that brief period he had sunk into a deep sleep. It went to show how exhausted he was. In fact, he hardly found the strength to climb out of the car. He felt dizzy as he headed for the school gate and bumped into Miss Vriends.

'Excuse me,' they said simultaneously.

'Miss Vriends, what a coincidence,' Douwe said in surprise. 'Just the person I need.'

'I'm sorry, sir,' she said, 'what did you say?'

'Hello,' Douwe said waving his hands in front of him, 'recognize me? Pieter Douwe from the museum?'

'Yes, of course. Mister Douwe. I'm ever so sorry, but I was still in hospital with my thoughts. One of my pupils met with an accident.'

'I hope it's not too bad.'

'O no, quite the contrary. He has regained consciousness. But do tell me, what did you want to see me for?'

'I wanted to ask you about your visit to the museum the other day. There was this boy who stayed behind in the Bruegel hall as you were leaving.'

'Ben Teugels you mean?'

'Rather short, red hair.'

'That's the one. How odd that you should ask for him just now,' Vriends said.

'Why is that?'

'Because he's sleeping, if you can call it *sleeping*, and I just cannot wake him up. I've tried everything, from a wet towel to a slap in the face. But he keeps on tossing and turning like he's having a terrible nightmare. And he doesn't stop begging. Most of what he says is gibberish, but one sentence keeps coming back: 'Please Freddy, bring me back.'

'Who's Freddy?' asked Douwe.

'He's the boy in hospital. He's Ben's best friend. He was unconscious after he got hit by a car in Nationale straat yesterday. But as I said, he's awake now. So, I asked him about Ben.'

'And what did he say?'

'I couldn't believe my ears. According to Freddy Ben is stuck in a painting.'

'In a Bruegel,' Douwe said.

'However do you know?' Vriends asked in surprise.

'Bring me to him. I think I can explain.'

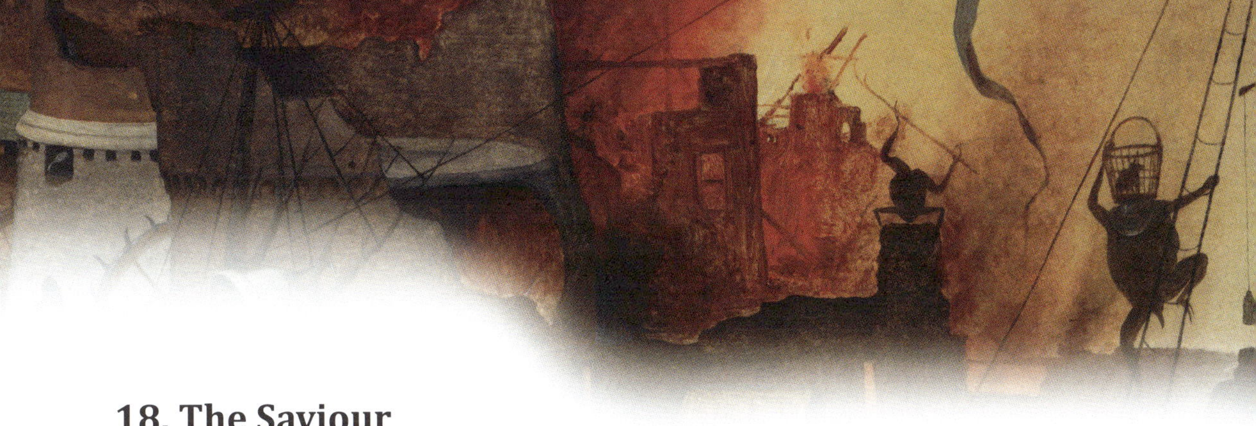

18. The Saviour

My voice was hoarse from begging, but I kept at it.

'Please, Freddy, bring me back. Please, Freddy...'

I only kept quiet every time a grotesque creature appeared on top of the hill, its misshapen form silhouetted against the red glow. I crouched deeper into the ditch and watched as the monster passed me by. Then I started imploring Freddy again to pull me out of there.

I don't know how long I had been hiding, when I heard shuffling nearby. I shut my eyes tight and clasped my hands to my mouth to keep from crying out. Something was sniffing its way towards me. It stopped in front of me and gave a soft yelp. It was a sound I instantly recognized.

'Max?' I whispered. I looked up slowly and could not believe my eyes. There stood Max, the white patch on his breast faintly visible in the darkness.

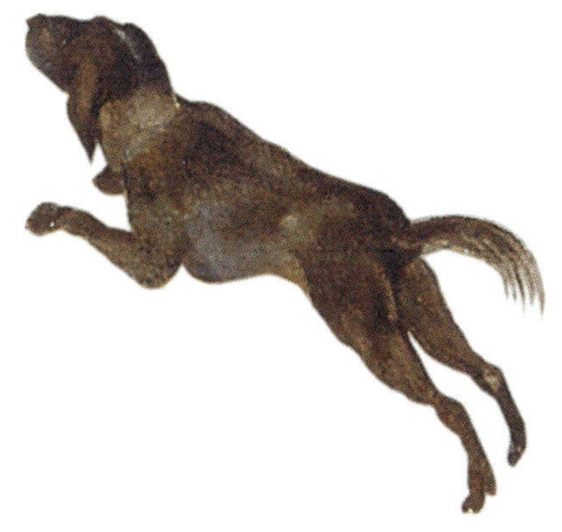

'Is that you, Max?'

He barked his so familiar bark.

'Here, Max,' I said sitting up.

He jumped into my arms, his tail wagging like crazy, and licked my face. His rasping tongue, his rough fur, the smell of him, how I had missed all that. I said his name over and over again, just to savour it. 'Max! Max, my saviour! Good dog!'

It was sunrise when I followed Max into the maze of alleyways. Without hesitation he turned left and right. Suddenly he stopped dead in his tracks. Huddled in a corner the bearded cripple lay sleeping, his red helmet by his side. Tied around it was the colourful shoelace. But there was no sign of my dummy stone. Of course, I thought, the cripples had only been after the shoelace in the first place. What use was a pebble stone to them? They must have dropped it somewhere. I had to find

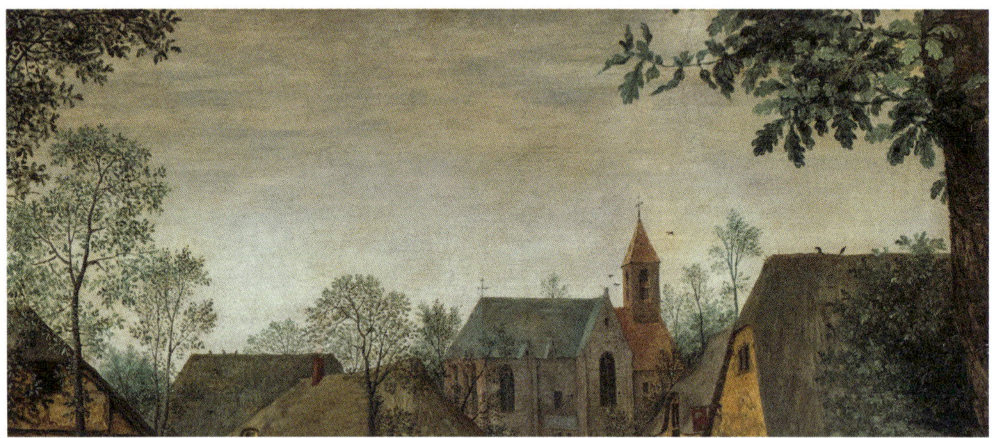

it, because without my dummy stone there was no way Freddy could ever pull me out of here. I had Max smell the shoelace.

'Help me find the pebble stone, Max,' I said. As I searched the area, Max kept sniffing where the cripple slept. When he barked, the cripple started and without opening his eyes he shooed the dog away. Max drew back and kept quiet until the cripple had settled himself to go back to sleep. Then he barked again. This time the cripple sat up swearing and threw a stone at the dog. Max caught it in mid-air, came over to me and dropped it at my feet. It was my dummy stone.

The village was still asleep as Max and I walked its streets to where the peasant wedding had been. Outside the barn the bagpiper was snoring. The table behind him was strewn with toppled jugs and near empty plates. I wolfed down the leftover pie and drank the dregs of beer from the few jugs that were still standing.

Now that I had finally reached my destination I suddenly felt dog-tired. I wanted to go and lie down in the barn, ready to be pulled out of there. 'Come, Max,' I said feeling for my dummy-stone in my pocket. But Max stayed put, his tail wagging. 'What's the matter, Max?' But I already knew the answer. From here on we would be going our separate ways. He couldn't go where I was going. Because there he was dead, snatched from my life. Each and every day I had felt the pain of that sudden loss. Now at last, I was able to do what I didn't get to do then: say goodbye to him properly. I took his head between my hands and looked into his deep brown eyes.

'Farewell Max, my faithful friend. Maybe we'll meet again, in another life.' And then I let go of him. He barked one more time and took off into the sunlight.

19. The Key

I felt someone pulling the pebble stone and, in a flash, I was back in my bed.

'What's this then?' a man's voice asked.

'That's strange. He didn't have that on him when I left him earlier.'

Wasn't that Miss Vriends speaking? I opened my eyes.

'Well, well,' she said. 'Look who's back among the living. Hello, Ben, awake at last?'

There was an old man beside her who was examining my dummy stone.

'You had me quite worried there, Ben,' Vriends said. 'You must have had a terrible nightmare the way you tossed and turned. Every now and then you screamed and covered your ears but there was no way I could wake you. And you kept repeating the same words: 'Freddy, please bring me back.'

'Freddy?' I croaked.

'Oh, I'm sorry. I should have put your mind at ease straight away,' she said. 'Freddy's regained consciousness. He has to stay in hospital for a while, but he'll be alright.'

I was so relieved I could have kissed her.

'How did you come by this pebble stone?' the old man cut in, looking at me with bloodshot eyes. His face seemed vaguely familiar.

'You remember mister Douwe, don't you?' Vriends said. 'The museum attendant?'

That's right. 'The Bruegel man,' I said.

That seemed to please him because his tone of voice became friendlier. 'Tell me, Ben. It's Ben, right? Tell me where you got this from?'

'I found it.'

'You found it! Well, that's quite a feat. It's not every day someone finds something from the sixteenth century.'

'The sixteenth century?' Vriends exclaimed.

'Yes,' I said to impress her, 'it says 1557 on one side of the stone and Max on the other.'

'Max? Wasn't that your dog's name?' she said.

'Yes, it was.' I was pleased she remembered. 'Actually, it was my dog who found it. A sixteenth century dog tag with his name on it. Go figure!' I was babbling away by now. And the old man, Douwe, kept me going.

'Where exactly did your dog find the stone?'

'Up in my aunt's attic.'

'You don't say. And where does she live, this aunt of yours?'

'In Kaasstraat.'

'And was the pie at the Peasant Wedding any good?'

'The best I ever ate.'

My words hung in the air. It was only when I saw Miss Vriends' jaw drop, her eyes like saucers, that I realized I had betrayed myself.

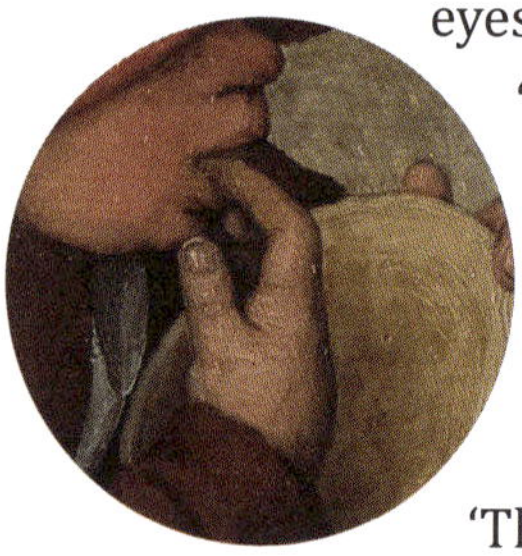

'Ben?' she said in utter disbelief.

I turned red in the face.

'Yes,' said Douwe, 'he's the intruder in Bruegel's paintings.'

'But how did he...?' Miss Vriends was so shocked she couldn't finish her sentences.

'The dog tag is the key, you see. Bruegel must have made it when he lived in the house where Ben's aunt now lives.'

'So that missing plate...' Miss Vriends stammered.

'That was Ben's doing,' Douwe said.

'But then... your composition, it wasn't... Ben Teugels! Pulling my leg like that.'

'He fooled the whole world. International crime syndicates, my foot! A mere twelve-year-old. What a joke!' Douwe burst out laughing.

'And Oh!' Vriends cried as another thought hit her. 'That book on Bruegel. I almost fell off my chair when you showed up in the library. It all adds up now.'

'I'm afraid, miss,' I said hesitantly, 'the book is a bit overdue.'

'A bit overdue,' she said and started laughing too. Soon the three of us were in stitches.

'I thought you would be angry,' I said when we were done laughing.

'I am too!' Douwe said. 'I'm very angry you made such a mess of my Bruegels. But I must admit I'm quite jealous too.'

'What do you mean, jealous?' Vriends asked.

'Our boy Ben was able to do what I could only dream of for forty-odd years: get into Bruegel's world. That would be heaven for me. Only, I'd keep my hands to myself.'

There was a knock at the door. The Letter stuck his head in. 'Excuse me, miss Vriends,' he said, 'but the police are here.'

20. Coward

The police! This time I was done for.

'Show them in, De Letter,' said Vriends apparently at ease.

In came two men who seemed like characters straight out of a detective movie. One was young and athletic, the other old and fat. And just like in the movies they flashed their police badges as they presented themselves.

'Detective inspector Beckx,' the elder one said.

'Detective sergeant Peters,' said the other.

'Gentlemen,' Douwe said, 'I can't say it's a pleasure to see you again. What brings you here, if I may ask?'

'That's precisely what we wanted to ask you, mister Douwe,' said Beckx.

I held my breath. Was the old man going to betray me?

'I've come for the boy,' he said.

There it was. I already saw myself behind bars.

'I've come to see how he's doing,' the old man added. 'His friend had an accident in Nationale Straat, not far from where I live.'

'We know where you live, Douwe. We searched your place and found the collection of Bruegel copies you made.'

'They stink!' Douwe said. 'I tried and tried again but Bruegel is...'

'I do the talking, Douwe,' Beckx cut in. 'Peters, check that accident. And who may you be, madam?'

'I'm looking after the boy,' Vriends said. If it was a slip of the tongue it was the loveliest I had ever heard. 'I mean, Ben is a pupil of mine,' she added blushing.

'There was an accident, sir,' said Peters who had called the station.

'Okay,' Beckx said, 'the lady can stay with the boy. Douwe, you're coming with us.'

I wish I could say that I jumped up and told the police it was all my fault. But I held my mouth like the coward I was.

'Inspector,' Douwe sighed, 'the last time you arrested me, you had to let me go for lack of evidence. I hope you have more solid proof this time, because I'm too tired to play your little games.'

'Little games?!' Beckx cried. 'This is an international police operation under my command. We knew you were the mastermind. So, we followed your every move since your release. Your trip to Vienna. Your secret calls to your accomplices all over the world. They are all being rounded up and put behind bars as we speak.

So, mister Douwe, do you still think we are playing little games?'

This time I did come forward. I couldn't let all those people pay for what was my doing. 'It's all my fault!' I exclaimed.

The detectives looked at me in surprise.

'You have to excuse him, detectives,' Vriends said, 'but the poor boy keeps blaming himself for his friend's accident.'

'The police report was clear, buddy,' Peters said. 'You are not to blame.'

'What the boy needs is rest,' Beckx said.

'So do I,' said Douwe who suddenly looked old and tired. 'You go ahead and lock me up so that I can have some rest at last.'

Detective sergeant Peters reached for his handcuffs.

'Can't we do without these, please?' Douwe pleaded.

'It's okay, Peters,' said Beckx. 'He won't run far.'

21. Reunion

As promised miss Vriends took me to hospital to see Freddy. 'To cheer you up,' she'd said. And I could do with some cheering up. Because every passing hour I felt more and more guilty about letting the old museum attendant take the blame for my misdeeds.

Freddy, his arm in plaster at an angle, seemed to be greeting us from afar. With his bandaged head reclining in a mountain of pillows he reminded me of a drunken king with a lopsided crown. It was a funny sight, but I did not dare to laugh. I was afraid I would start crying as well, for sheer joy at having my friend back.

'Hey,' was all I was able to say.

'Hey,' Freddy said.

There was an awkward silence.

It was Miss Vriends who broke the ice. 'Don't you think Freddy looks well, Ben?'

'He's lost weight,' I said.

'I did not eat for several days,' he said.

'Can you believe it,' Miss Vriends said in mock surprise. 'Freddy didn't eat for days and yet he's still alive.'

That made us laugh and the tension was gone. As we were telling Freddy everything that had happened while he was unconscious, it suddenly dawned on me Douwe had kept my dummy-stone to himself.

'That's why he asked the policemen not to handcuff him,' I said. 'He still held the stone in his hand.'

By the time visiting hours were over, the three of us had come to a decision. The next morning miss Vriends would take me to the police station and I would confess to everything. But things turned out otherwise.

That evening I sat with the boys, watching the TV-news. Since the accident they left me in peace. There was a report of some cycling event and Sebastian was all ears. He knew a lot about everything, but he knew everything about cycling. I no longer knew what to think of him. When I returned from hospital he was the first one to come and ask how Freddy was doing. And didn't he escort me to school after the accident?

'What are you gawking at me for, Redhead?' Sebastian asked.

'Sorry, I didn't mean to stare. It's just that you're less of a bastard than I thought you were,' I said with a grin.

'Why thank you, Redhead.' It was the first time we smiled at each other.

'But why are you so dead set on being the best at everything?'

'Because I want to be a cycling champion.'

'A cycling champion?' I said laughingly. 'You're kidding me.'

'You sound just like my father. He wants me to be a surgeon, just like him. We made a deal, he and I. If I can prove I have the brains to be a surgeon, if I get the best marks for every course the whole year long, he'll buy me that racing bike I've set my mind on. And then I can cycle as much as I want during the holidays.'

And that's when I heard Pieter Douwe's name being mentioned on TV. They were showing a picture of him. I grabbed the remote and pressed the volume button.

'...who was arrested yesterday,' the newscaster's voice blared through the recreation room.

'Are you deaf?' Jeff shouted, trying to take the remote from me.

'Let him,' Sebastian said.

I turned down the volume a little.

'... presumed to be the mastermind behind the Bruegel Mystery, was found dead in his cell. Reportedly, the cause of death is a heart attack. On the body of the deceased the police found a note with a message as mysterious as the Bruegel Mystery itself.'

The camera zoomed in on a piece of paper. On it, in shaky handwriting, were two short sentences:

THE KEY IS MINE. I WILL BE FINE.

22. A Finger in the Pie

When the world woke up the next morning all the vandalized Bruegels had been restored to their original state. In *The Peasant Wedding* the large tray counted ten plates again. In *The Peasant Dance* the jug had found its way back to the table behind the bagpiper. The sausage fence in *Lazy-Luscious-Land* showed no more holes and, on the roof, no more pies were missing.

'This is Douwe's doing of course,' said Freddy. Miss Vriends and I were sitting by his hospital bed for a crisis meeting. 'He used the stone to go and set things right.'

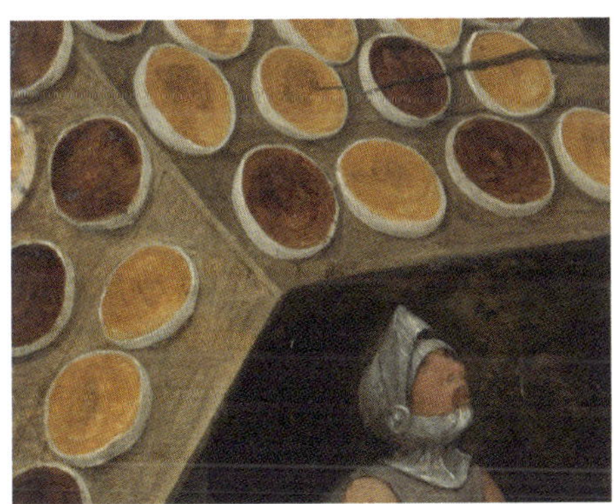

'And he made it disappear,' Vriends added, 'to make sure no intruder will ever get into Bruegel land again.'

'He will be fine there,' I said. 'He's gone to his heaven.'

'Come to think of it, Ben,' Freddy said, 'technically speaking all evidence against you has been wiped away. So, does it still make sense to go to the police and confess to everything?'

That gave us something to talk about. Ultimately, we decided to keep it all to ourselves. It was to be our secret.

For a few days there was a new run on the Bruegels. But it was short-lived because in the end the paintings had gone back to what they always had been. The world media found other fish to fry. The police investigation, following the death of their main suspect, petered out. And soon the Bruegel Mystery drifted into oblivion.

There was, however, one thing that still worried me, so I went to the museum to put my mind at ease. The new woman attendant was clearly surprised to see a boy who came to look at the Bruegels all by himself. She kept an eye on me as I made a beeline for *The Massacre of the Innocents*. The horsemen stood as still as ever. I singled out the brute who had kept coming after me. He stood back in line and no longer looked at me.

'Phew!' I said.

'No blowing on the paintings, please,' said the attendant.

It sounded like Douwe speaking. I still felt his presence, not in the hall but in the paintings. As if he was watching me while I counted the plates in *The Peasant Wedding*. For a second I even thought I saw a glimpse of him, that was impossible, of course. Douwe had said he would keep his hands to himself. And yet, if one looked closely enough, that spot in the first plate to the right, wasn't that the imprint of a finger in the pie?

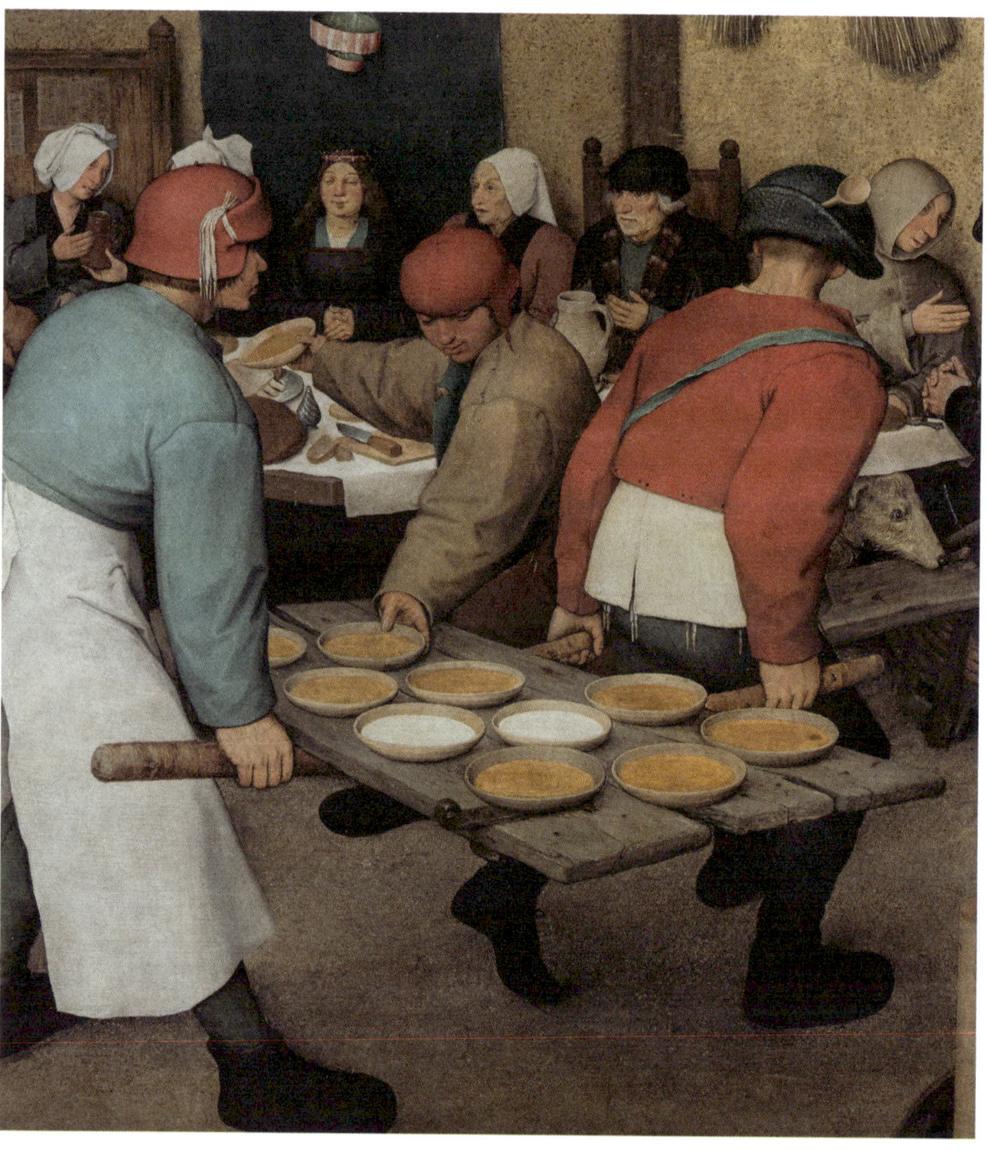

23. Rose

June came and the exams. Sebastian came out first for all subjects. Only for composition did he have to share first place with me.

And then the school year was over. Prince Albert's closed its doors for the summer holidays. The driveway was busy with parents coming to fetch their children. Boys were saying goodbye. There was hugging and laughter and cars honking as they drove off.

'So, Ben, all set to go?' Miss Vriends said as I put my trunk in the boot of her car.

'Yes, miss.'

'I hope you're not going to call me Miss all summer,' she said laughing. I was to spend part of the holidays with her. That had been agreed with aunt Jo, who couldn't possibly take two months off to look after me in that small house in the city. And miss Vriends had time and room to spare. She lived in the countryside in a spacious house with a big garden. And she had two dogs!

'Just call me Rose, all right?'

'Yes, miss. I mean Rose.' And I silently repeated her name to taste how sweet it was.

'Goodbye, Little Red Riding Hood,' Freddy called out as I got into the car.

I stuck my head out of the window. 'Goodbye, Freddybear.'

It turned out Vriends did not live far from Freddy's parents. And he and I had agreed to visit one another at least once a week.

'Don't forget to drop by, Ben!' Freddy shouted as the car got moving.

Through the rear window I watched Prince Albert's growing smaller.

'You're so quiet, Ben. Don't worry, it will all work out.' She brushed her hand through my hair. 'Everything will turn out right, my boy.'

Antwerp today

And everything turned out right. The summer of '89 was one of the happiest in my life. I only slept twice in Kaasstraat and aunt Jo visited Miss Rose only once. After that my aunt and I hardly saw each other again. Rose became my new mother, her house my new home.

Freddy and I spent most of the summer vacation together. We made long walks with the dogs. At the end of the holidays Freddy had lost quite a few pounds. He's still my best friend and when I asked him to be godfather to my new-born son, he cried.

It feels like yesterday that Daan was born. On the very day that Sebastian became world champion for the third time in a row. And now my son is already turning six. Today he will finally get his puppy.

He woke me up at 7 a.m. asking if it wasn't high time we went to the pet shop. Because soon the whole family would arrive to see his new dog. Grandma Rose would be there. And uncle Freddybear, of course. What if they were all there and his doggy wasn't?

So here we stand before the closed shutter of the pet shop. There's already a lot of coming and going in Schildersstraat, because today the great Bruegel exposition will open its doors.

Daan is fiddling with the dog tag we made for his puppy. He also wanted one with a pebble stone. And so, the two of us went to Saint Anneke's Beach. As I sat and watched him pick up stones and throw them away, I noticed the perfect pebble stone lying right in front of me. It was black with a white vein in it, flat and smooth.

'I found one, papa,' he called out as he came running over.

I quickly pushed my stone halfway into the sand and put my feet around it.

'Look,' he said proudly, showing me a stone the size of my hand.

'That's exactly what we're looking for,' I said not to discourage him, 'but a bit smaller. Like these ones right here.'

As I moved my feet, he saw the black stone and pulled it out of the sand.

'O, that looks like a beauty. Can I see it?'

He radiated as I examined the stone. 'Well done, Daan! I'll tell you something. A good dog tag must be the size of the puppy's paw imprint and fit snugly in the closed hand of its master. So, open your hand.'

Solemnly I put the pebble stone in the palm of his hand. He briefly looked at it and slowly closed his hand.

'It fits,' he said in a whisper.

'Good. Now all you need to do is choose a name for your dog and we'll have it engraved on the stone.'

'I already have a name, papa,' he said implying I should have guessed by now. 'I'm calling him Max, that way he's also a bit yours again.'

'How much longer?' he asks impatiently.

I check my watch. 'Three more minutes.'

In recent months we've stood here so often to look at the puppies, the shopkeeper knows us by name. Each time Daan declared with conviction his hadn't arrived yet. But today it will, that he's firmly convinced of.

The shutter creaks.

'The shop opens up!' Daan cries. He kneels down and tries to look through the widening gap. Together with the shutter his head comes up. And then a jolt goes through his little body.

'I can see him,' he says breathlessly. He pulls my pants. 'Papa, come and look. Max is there.'

Passers-by look at me as I kneel down next to my son. On the other side of the glass is a baby Belgian Shepherd. It's got a white spot on its breast. Daan taps on the window and the puppy puts a front paw against the glass. He places the pebble stone against it.

'It fits,' he says in a voice brimming with happiness.

'Good morning, mister Teugels,' says the shopkeeper. I quickly get up. 'So, the old man was right,' he says with an amused look on his face. 'He said you would be here first thing in the morning.'

I feel a shiver down my spine. 'Which old man?'

'He said you'd know who he was. It was no effort to bring the puppy. He had to be here anyway. 'To keep an eye on things, what with all these people coming to see my Bruegels.' That's how he said it. 'My Bruegels.''

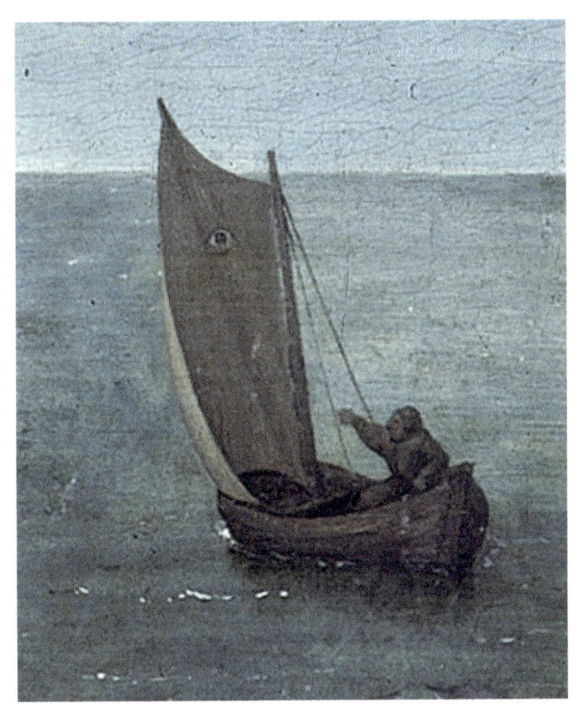

Colofon

AUTHOR
Luc Verreth

LAYOUT AND TYPESETTING
Ann Walkers

PRINTED
Graphius

RESPONSIBLE PUBLISHER
BAI (Kontich)

ILLUSTRATIONS: PIETER BRUEGEL
Cover, p. 29, 30, 35, 37, 48, 66, 72: The Peasant Wedding, Vienna, Kunsthistorisches Museum
p. 6: Baasrode, bpk | Kupferstichkabinett, SMB | Volker-H. Schneider
p. 12, 14, 27: The Hunters in the Snow, Vienna, Kunsthistorisches Museum
p. 15, 16, 26, 56, 63: Massacre of the Innocents, Vienna, Kunsthistorisches Museum
p. 18-19, 21, 22, 77: Proverbs, bpk | Gemäldegalerie, SMB | Jörg P. Anders
p. 38, 41, 51, 64: The Peasant Dance, Vienna, Kunsthistorisches Museum
p. 46, 50, 53, 71: The Land of Cockaigne, München, Alte Pinakothek
p. 31: The Harvesters, New York, The Metropolitan Museum of Art | © Scala, Florence
p. 55: The Cripples, Paris, Musée du Louvre | Photo © RMN-Grand Palais (musée du Louvre), Tony Querrec
p. 58-59, 60, 63: Dulle Griet (Mad Meg) Antwerp, Museum Mayer van den Bergh | Photo: KIK-IRPA

ISBN 9789085867722
D/2018/5751/21